WEAVING FAITH AND EXPERIENCE

Weaving Faith and Experience

A

WOMAN'S

PERSPECTIVE

Patricia Cooney Hathaway

ST. ANTHONY MESSENGER PRESS
Cincinnati, Ohio

Scripture passages have been taken from *New Revised Standard Version Bible,* copyright
©1989 by the Division of Christian Education of the National Council of the Churches
of Christ in the U.S.A., and used by permission. All rights reserved.

Excerpts from *The Seasons of a Woman's Life* by Daniel J. Levinson. Copyright © 1997 by
Ballantine Books, a division of Random House, Inc. "The Contemplation of Wisdom"
from *Collected Poems (1930-1993)* copyright © 1972 by May Sarton. Used by permission
of W. W. Norton & Company, Inc. From *Seasons* by Anita Spencer. Copyright © 1982 by
Paulist Press.

Book and cover design by Mark Sullivan
Cover image © Fenghui | Dreamstime.com

LIBRARY OF CONGRESS CATALOGING-IN-PUBLICATION DATA
Cooney Hathaway, Patricia.
Weaving faith and experience : a woman's perspective / Patricia Cooney Hathaway.
p. cm. — (Called to holiness)
Includes bibliographical references.
ISBN 978-0-86716-904-1 (pbk. : alk. paper) 1. Catholic women—Religious life. 2.
Psychology and religion. I. Title.

BX2353.C66 2010
248.8'43088282—dc22
2010000118

ISBN 978-0-86716-904-1

Published by St. Anthony Messenger Press
28 W. Liberty St.
Cincinnati, OH 45202
www.SAMPBooks.org
www.CalledtoHoliness.org

Printed in the United States of America.

Printed on acid-free paper.

10 11 12 13 14   5 4 3 2 1

CONTENTS

ABOUT THE SERIES

I wish to acknowledge the support and encouragement of an organization of philanthropists: Foundations and Donors Interested in Catholic Activities (FADICA). In January of 2005, I was invited to speak before this organization at a conference entitled Women of Faith. The discussion explored the many contributions of women to Roman Catholic ministry, church leadership and theology.

The members of FADICA heard my appeal for a renewed focus on women's spirituality in the context of significant religious change during the twentieth century and the pressing challenges of the twenty-first. The need for a creative, solidly grounded, and theologically sophisticated spirituality available in an accessible form for all Christian women seemed obvious. Follow-up conversations by the FADICA board, ably led by Frank Butler, led to a proposal from Fairfield University for a series of books on women's spirituality. Thus, FADICA, Fairfield University, and St. Anthony Messenger Press formed a collaborative partnership to produce seven volumes under the title *Called to Holiness: Spirituality for Catholic Women.*

I wish to thank individuals and foundations whose generosity made this collaborative venture possible. These include the Amature Family Foundation, the AMS Fund, the Cushman Foundation, the Mary J. Donnelly Foundation, George and Marie Doty, Mrs. James Farley, the Robert and Maura Burke Morey Charitable Trust, Maureen O'Leary, Ann Marie Paine and the Raskob Foundation for Catholic Activities. I wish to extend a word of thanks and praise to the entire FADICA membership, whose conscientious, quiet and loving participation in shaping the life of the church has been an inspiration.

The focus of this series is spirituality. Its interest is women of all back-
grounds: rich and poor; married and single; white, black and brown;
gay and straight; those who are biological mothers and those who are
mothers in other senses. There will be volumes on grassroots theology,
family life, prayer, action for justice, grieving, young adult issues, wisdom years and Hispanic heritage. I hope all the volumes in this series
will deepen and shape your own spiritual life in creative ways, as you
engage with the theology of our rich, two-thousand-year-old
Christian tradition.

Women's spiritualities are lived in light of their concrete, specific
experiences of joy and struggle; ecstasy and despair; virtue and vice;
work and leisure; family and friends; embodiment and sexuality; tears
and laughter; sickness and health; sistering and mothering. These volumes are for women and men from all walks of life, whether they are
new to the spiritual journey or old hands, affluent, middle-class or
poor. Included in the circle we call church are persons from every
country on the planet, some at the center, others at the margins or
even beyond.

The time is ripe for "ordinary" women to be doing theology. The
first and second waves of the women's movement in the nineteenth
and twentieth centuries provided a valiant and solid foundation for
the third wave which will mark, and be marked by, the world of the
early twenty-first century. Changes and developments from one generation to the next makes our heads spin. Younger women readers are
likely to be already grooming the soil for a fourth wave of Christian
spirituality done by and for women. Women have always loved God,

served others and struggled with sin, but the historical context has been less than friendly in terms of women's dignity, acknowledgment of female gifts and empowerment by church and society. In a time of growing emphasis on the role of clergy, and the backlash against women in society, the voices of the laity—especially the voices of women—are needed more than ever.

The Greek language has two words for time. *Chronos* points to the time signaled by the hands on the clock—for example, it is a quarter past two. *Kairos* points to time that is ripe, a moment pregnant with possibility. As Christian women, we live in a time rightly described as *kairos*. It is a time that calls us, demands of us renewed energy, reflection and commitment to attend to and help each other grow spiritually as we seek to love ourselves and the world. At this point in history, the fruit of women's struggle includes new self-awareness, self-confidence and self-respect. More and more women are beginning to see just how lovable and capable they are. The goal of the Christian life has always been to lay down our lives in love for the other, but the particular ways this vocation is lived out differ from era to era and place to place. Women's ability to voice with confidence the phrase, "I am a theologian" at the beginning of the twenty-first century means something it could not have meant even fifty years ago.

Those who were part of the early waves of feminism celebrate the hard-won accomplishments of the women's movement and know that this work needs to be taken up by future generations. Young women in their twenties and thirties are often unaware of past efforts that brought about more dignity and freedom for women. Women have opened many doors, but many remain closed. The media have recently explored the plight of Hindu widows in India; less publicized is that women in the United States still earn only seventy-seven cents for every dollar earned by their male counterparts. We must be vigilant and continue to act for decades to come in order to secure our accomplishments thus far and make further inroads toward the creation of a just, egalitarian world. Those who sense that the women's movement is in a doldrums inspire us to renew the enthusiasm and dedication of our foremothers.

When we cast our eye beyond the women of our own nation, it takes but a split-second to realize that the majority of the world's poor and oppressed are women. A quick visit to the Women's Human Rights Watch Web site reveals the breadth and depth of women's oppression across the globe from poverty and domestic abuse to sex slavery. Most women (and their children) do not have enough to eat, a warm, dry place to sleep or access to education. Female babies are more at risk than male babies. Women, more than men, lack the protection of the law and the respect of their communities. The double-standard in sexual matters affects women in harmful ways in all cultures and economic groups across the globe.

For all of these reasons it is not just important—but pressing, crucial, urgent—that all women of faith own the title "theologian" and shape this role in light of each woman's unique set of characteristics, context, relationships and spiritualities. We are theologians when we sort through our experience and the great and small problems of our time through reflection on Scripture or the words of a mystic or theologian. The images of God that emerged for Paul, Augustine or Catherine of Siena provide guidance, but their theology cannot ever be a substitute for our own. Theology helps us shape what we think about God, justice, love, the destiny of humanity and the entire universe in a way that is relevant to the specific issues facing us in the twenty-first century. The call to spiritual depths and mystical heights has never been more resounding.

Elizabeth A. Dreyer
Series Editor

"I came that they may have life, and have it abundantly."
—John 10:10

Setting the Stage

Many years ago when I was teaching at Marygrove College, I came to the realization that spiritual and psychological issues were inextricably interwoven in our lives. That insight influenced my future as a theologian, teacher, spiritual director, and writer. During those years many women came to me for counseling and spiritual direction. I became aware that when someone came to me with a psychological issue, there was often a spiritual dimension to it as well. Likewise, when someone came to me with a spiritual issue, there was almost always a psychological component to it. For example, if a woman was struggling with an image of God as a distant, aloof father that blocked her ability to pray, that image often had its origins in her relationship with her own father. With this new awareness, I decided to offer a course on the stages of human and spiritual development. The course was helpful to students for two reasons. First, it related to their personal lives; second, it linked several sets of very significant components of their development that are often placed in opposition to each other: body and spirit, nature and grace, human and spiritual development, psychology and religion, church and world. When I joined the faculty at Sacred Heart Major Seminary, I knew it was essential that seminarians and lay students, who were preparing for ministry in the church, have the opportunity for such a course. It would provide them with insight into their own development as well as help them better understand the women and men they would serve in their ministries. A document from the Second Vatican Council, *Gaudium et Spes* (The Church in the Modern World), provided an important endorsement of the role of psychology in the spiritual life for those students who were hesitant to acknowledge its value.

> In pastoral care sufficient use should be made, not only of theological principles, but also of the findings of secular sciences, especially psychology and sociology; in this way the faithful will be brought to a purer and more mature life of faith.[1]

I soon received invitations to give workshops and conferences on this material throughout the diocese. On a number of occasions, I was asked to speak about the interweaving of women's human and spiritual journeys.

I chose the title, "Seasons of a Woman's Life, Seasons of a Woman's Faith," to describe these conferences with several goals in mind—goals that remain in place as I write this book. First, I wanted to see if the theory of adult development described in Dr. Daniel Levinson's book *Seasons of a Woman's Life* accurately described women's experience and was compatible with a Christian view of the human person. Second, I wanted to explore whether it provided a helpful description of the landscape of adult life within which grace works. The famous thirteenth-century Dominican theologian Thomas Aquinas taught that grace builds on and through nature; that is, grace, the self-communication of God's very being, works from *within* our human nature and our life experiences to draw us to God as the fulfillment of all our desires. Third, I wanted women to become familiar with the wisdom of the church's spiritual tradition on mysticism and spirituality. Many of us have the false impression that the lives and writings of saints who lived many years ago cannot possibly have anything to say to us today—a perception that I hope to show is far from the truth. Through the life stories and writings of such spiritual giants as Teresa of Avila, John of the Cross, and Thérèse of Lisieux, I explore the interweaving of the human and spiritual journey. I hope this endeavor will enable you to gain insight and practical help in your journey to wholeness and holiness.

The term *holy* derives from the Anglo-Saxon *hal* which means "whole" or "well." This meaning suggests that as we grow in holiness, we should also be growing in wholeness and health. The interrelationship between the two is expressed clearly by psychiatrist and spiritual writer Gerald May. He states that the issue of how psychology and spirituality interrelate in the contemporary world is one of the most pressing challenges we face today.

> Many of us expect science to provide us with the whys and what-fors, with some sense of meaning or belonging. Science cannot do this for us. While it can lead up to the ultimate questions, it cannot answer them. That has been and continues to be the domain of religion.... It does no good to blur the boundaries that exist between the two in the name of wholeness or integration. Better to walk their rugged interfaces.[2]

The method of this book respects the boundaries that exist between psychology and spirituality. It puts psychology in the service of spirituality; that is, a theory of human development is not an end in itself; rather, it provides the landscape within which grace—God's presence within us—works. Since spirituality and psychology have different goals, they can be beneficial to each other.

The discipline of psychology studies the human mind and behavior for the purpose of healing and health. It seeks to help a person answer some of life's basic questions: Who am I? Who am I with? Where am I going in terms of a life plan? What aids or blocks my growth? Whether we are aware of it or not, the language of psychology is in the air we breathe and informs how we access ourselves and others. Spirituality deals with these same questions through the lens of our relationship with God and others in faith. It recognizes a sacred dimension to life and often looks to a religious tradition to provide a roadmap of meaning and value around questions related to the ultimate concerns of life: Is God a personal God who is invested in my life? Do I have a personal destiny related to God? What is the meaning of suffering? What is my fate after death?

This book pursues an interpretation of adult development, then, in which God's grace can be discovered at work within the landscape of psychological growth. The challenges, crises, and tasks of human development become the context within which grace works to bring us to transforming union with God. We will proceed as life normally does. First, we will look at our human experience. Then we will ask the religious question: Where is God in this experience? How has this experience been a catalyst for spiritual as well as human growth?

Before we begin a study of women's seasons of faith and life with an emphasis on the middle years, I want to set the stage with important background in the areas of psychology and spirituality.

Seasons of a Woman's Life

While the study of childhood and adolescent development has been around for decades, the study of adult development is relatively new. At the age of forty-seven, Levinson began his study of adulthood for personal reasons—he wanted to know if there was life after forty! He felt that the wish to learn more about the possibilities of personal growth during the middle years was hampered by the fear that careful scrutiny would reveal only decline and restriction. Thus, the great silence about the experience of being an adult.

He began his study by asking the following questions: What does it mean to be an adult? What are the root issues of adult life—the essential problems and satisfactions, the sources of disappointment, grief, and fulfillment? And finally, is there an underlying order in the progression of our lives through the adult years as there is in childhood and adolescence? His research, based on a study of men, *The Seasons of a Man's Life* (1978), and a study of women, *The Seasons of a Woman's Life* (1996), suggests that there is a human life cycle that is lived uniquely by each person. He also posits that women go through the same developmental periods as men and at the same ages, but in partially different ways that reflect differences in biology and social circumstances.[3]

Levinson's sensitivity to gender is one of the reasons I was attracted to his work. He was aware that for centuries male experience had been viewed as normative for human experience. He learned, through listening to women's life stories, how deeply gender-specific expectations affected women's development, maturity, and personal happiness. Consequently, the primary aim of his book on women was to explore women's lives with the hope of helping them to better understand themselves and to improve their lives. The following chart (page xviii) visualizes the main components of Levinson's theory of adult development.

Levinson maintains that the life cycle evolves through a sequence of eras, each lasting roughly twenty-five years. The eras partially overlap so that a new one is getting underway as the previous one is being terminated. The sequence is as follows: Childhood and adolescence: birth to age twenty-two. Early adulthood: age seventeen to forty-five. Middle adulthood: age forty to sixty-five. Late adulthood: age sixty-five-plus.

Levinson's main focus is on the developmental periods over the course of early and middle adulthood from seventeen to sixty-five years of age. He refers to them as adult life structures which describe the underlying pattern of a person's life at a given time. He found that the life structure evolves through a sequence of alternating *stable* periods, each lasting some seven to ten years, followed by *transitional* periods in which we appraise the past and, if necessary, make changes for the future.

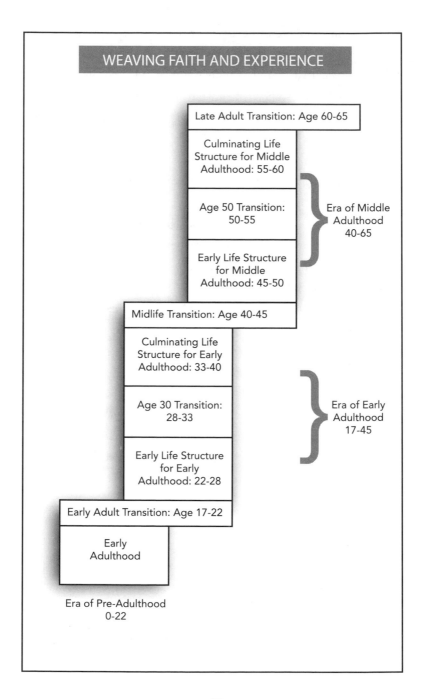

Levinson chose the image of seasons to describe his theory of psychological growth, because he assumed that everyone understands the connections between the seasons of the year and the seasons of the human life cycle. Spring is not intrinsically a better season than winter, nor is summer better than fall. On the contrary, each season has its own distinctive character, its own particular tone, and needs to be understood on its own terms. Spring is a time of blossoming, winter a time of death but also of rebirth and the start of a new cycle.

Whenever I have the opportunity to speak about the usefulness of stage development theory for understanding adult life, I always begin and end with a word of caution. At its best, a theory of adult development offers us a framework for insight and understanding regarding our own as well as others' life journeys. At its worst, it can be misused to box women and men into stages that disrespect the complexities as well as uniqueness of each individual life. Acknowledging that no theory can totally describe our life experience, we move forward, allowing Levinson's theory to shed light on the mysterious world of adulthood.

Seasons of a Woman's Faith

The spiritual life has been described by many images within our Christian tradition. One of the most dominant has been the *ladder*. Recall the hymn "We Are Climbing Jacob's Ladder": The image is one of ascent. It is hierarchical. A person advances from one level to another, from an imperfect to a more perfect state.

Another image that emerges in the Christian tradition is that of *journey*—the journey of our spiritual life; the journey of our relationship with God. This image reminds us that human life is not static. On the contrary, it is an ever-unfolding, dynamic process. We may be moving forward, retreating backward, getting lost, and finding our way again. We are never standing still. While the images of ladder and journey are helpful, the image of *seasons* appeals more to women today as a lens through which to better understand the stages of their spiritual development.

Our relationship with God has a seasonal quality to it. For example, we can speak of the spring of a newly discovered relationship with God; summer as a time of deeper reflection as to who God really is for us; autumn as a time for finding God in the midst of the successes and limitations of life; winter as a time of trustful faith as we seek God's blessing on our one and only life in the face of impending death. One season is not intrinsically better than another for our spiritual growth; each has its own beauty, challenges, and graces. Also, we can cycle through the seasons many times and not always in their natural order. Most importantly, maturity and growth in the spiritual life are no longer determined by how quickly we move up the ladder, but by how well we negotiate the challenges and invitations of each season. As personal relationships have their seasons—their ups and downs, peaks and valleys, periods of intimacy as well as periods of contention and dryness—so too does our relationship with God.

It is vitally important to point out that spiritual growth is not always in sync with human development. There are young women with a deep, mature spirituality, and older women who are very young in the spiritual life. God works with us, helping us grow and mature through each season—no matter the pattern of our lives. We need to remember that grace is ever capable of surprising us at any time.

A Scripture passage which illustrates this cooperative venture between God and each of us is the story of Jeremiah and the potter (Jeremiah 18:1–6):

> The word that came to Jeremiah from the Lord: "Come, go down to the potter's house, and there I will let you hear my words." So I went down to the potter's house, and there he was working at his wheel. The vessel he was making of clay was spoiled in the potter's hand, and he reworked it into another vessel, as seemed good to him.
>
> Then the word of the Lord came to me: Can I not do with you…just as this potter has done? says the Lord. Just like the clay in the potter's hand, so are you in my hand.

We are in God's hands. When we cooperate with God's invitation and guidance in our lives, God promises to work with us. When we go astray and resist God's grace, God continues to work with us, molding us and forming us into the women God desires us to become.

The interweaving of the human and spiritual dimensions of life is based on the Christian conviction that God's continual working with us on our journey toward transforming union does not develop apart from human life but within it. Too often, however, to paraphrase T.S. Eliot, we have the experience but miss the meaning. Why is that? Many of us were raised in a Catholic spirituality that taught us to find God in the sacred places and activities of our lives—liturgy, sacraments, devotions—such as the way of the cross, adoration of the blessed sacrament and so on. These spiritual practices were seen as the primary way to holiness. Without diminishing the importance of these sacred places and activities, the Second Vatican Council reminds us that all of life—family, work, social and political involvements—provide a context for God's visitations to us as well. The everyday successes and failures of each season of life can be invitations to a deeper relationship with God if we have the eyes to see. The ability to interpret our life experience within a Christian context depends upon the meaning we bring to faith.

The verb, *credo,* "I believe" comes from the Latin noun, *cor, cordis,* which means "heart," and the verb *do, dare,* which means "to give." Thus, the root meaning of "I believe" is "I set my heart on; I give my heart to." Taken in the context of the New Testament, "I believe" means I commit myself to God; I set my heart on God. Here faith is not static. We do not give our minds and hearts to God once and for all. On the contrary, faith is an ongoing experience of growth in our relationship with God. It involves many levels on which we meet God in praise, anger, disappointment, boredom, joy, gratitude, petition, and expectation. It also encompasses ever deeper levels of intentionality and commitment.

This book explores Christian faith as growth in a personal relationship with God, a falling in love with God that finds practical expression in the way we choose to live. This relationship—like every relationship in our lives—grows and deepens, or deteriorates and dies as we live through each season of life.

Weaving Faith and Experience: A Perspective on the Middle Years

What do you consider to be the challenges of your particular season of life? How do you describe your spirituality at this time of your life? Writing down the answers will help you to reflect on the interweaving of your human and spiritual journey. In the course of this book, I will share many responses of women to these questions as a powerful illustration of two important truths: First, our most personal human experience is also the most universal. In other words, we see ourselves in the stories of other women, and learn from them. Second, the answers women give to these questions illustrate clearly the interweaving of the human and spiritual journey during each season of life.

Since most of my experience has been with women in their middle years, this book will concentrate on the autumn and the beginning of the winter of life. However, these seasons will not be viewed in isolation. To split the life course into unconnected segments, without recognizing the place of each segment in the life cycle as a whole, is to risk fragmentation. Women are where they are in the autumn and winter of life because of dreams pursued, choices made, successes celebrated, and failures endured through the spring and summer of their lives. Thus, this book concentrates on understanding the relationship between faith and human experience during the middle years within the context of the whole life cycle.

I invite you to enter into each season of life as *your* life from *your* particular vantage point at the present time. As the following chart illustrates, each chapter explores the weaving of the human and faith dimensions of life's journey. The descriptive title of faith for each season—interpersonal, reflective, paradoxical, intentional, and trusting—emerged gradually from my pondering the stories of many women. I felt like the titles chose me rather than I chose them. So, if they fit your experience, fine. If not, then let God lead you along another path.

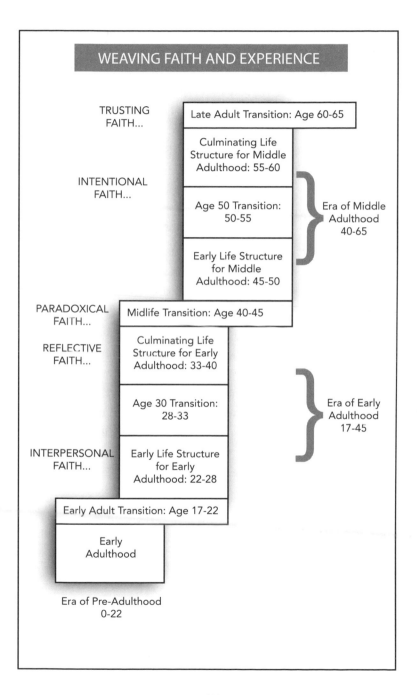

WEAVING FAITH AND EXPERIENCE

TRUSTING FAITH...

Late Adult Transition: Age 60-65

INTENTIONAL FAITH...

Culminating Life Structure for Middle Adulthood: 55-60

Age 50 Transition: 50-55

Early Life Structure for Middle Adulthood: 45-50

Era of Middle Adulthood 40-65

PARADOXICAL FAITH...

Midlife Transition: Age 40-45

REFLECTIVE FAITH...

Culminating Life Structure for Early Adulthood: 33-40

Age 30 Transition: 28-33

INTERPERSONAL FAITH...

Early Life Structure for Early Adulthood: 22-28

Era of Early Adulthood 17-45

Early Adult Transition: Age 17-22

Early Adulthood

Era of Pre-Adulthood 0-22

Chapter one combines the spring and summer of life as a backdrop for our exploration of the middle years. It looks at the first half of life as predominantly an outward journey and the spiritual enterprise as "waking up" to a personal, reflective relationship with God. Chapter two explores the decade of the forties by describing the characteristics and challenges of midlife. It suggests that the texture of faith at this time of life is paradoxical: How can new life emerge from what often feels like dying? Chapter three explores four polarities that take center stage during the middle years: Old/Young, Destruction/Creation, Masculine/Feminine, Attachment/Separation. It then examines a way of doing theology that helps us view the polarities within the context of an intentional faith. Finally, chapter four probes the challenges and invitations of the season of winter. It invites us to a trusting faith as we begin to renegotiate our past in the context of the present, and accept with gratitude our one and only life story.

Some women have told me they don't want to study the landscape of adult life; they are fearful about exploring too deeply God's invitation to "sell all and come follow me." Carl Jung, a twentieth-century psychiatrist who is considered the father of adult development, tells us that we have a choice: We can walk upright into the future or we can be dragged into it blindly. I invite you to walk upright with me down some of the roads that provide insight and direction for the adult journey of faith.

FOOD FOR THOUGHT

1. What do you consider to be the challenges of this time of your life?
2. How do you describe your spirituality at this time?

REFLECTION

God is with me, but more
God is within me, giving me existence
Let me dwell for a moment on God's
life-giving presence
in my body, my mind, my heart,
and in the whole of my life.[4]

—Sacred Space: The Prayer Book

PRAYER

Take, Lord, and receive all my liberty my memory, my understanding, and my whole will, all I have and possess. You gave it to me; to you, Lord, I return it. It is all yours: do with me entirely as you will.[5]

—Ignatius of Loyola

CHAPTER ONE

• THE SPRING AND SUMMER OF LIFE •

This Is Spirituality: Waking Up.[1]
—Meister Eckhart

We do not enter the middle years with a clean slate, so to speak, but as women formed by the dreams we pursued, choices we made, successes we celebrated, and wounds we endured during the spring and summer of life. This chapter explores the spring and summer of our lives as the backdrop for gaining insight into the opportunities, challenges, and graces of our middle years, which we explore in subsequent chapters.

Using the imagery of seasons, Levinson describes the spring of life, ages seventeen to twenty-eight, as a time of blossoming and new beginnings. It is a time full of promise and possibilities. The early adult transition, ages seventeen to twenty-two, affords young women the opportunity to imagine various future possibilities for themselves and the world. In this initial period of the early adult era, a crucial task is to form and live out a dream.[2]

The dream refers to a sense of self projected onto the adult world. It confirms the initial, though often tentative, resolution of the critical task of adolescence which is to develop a sense of identity. By *identity* I mean the process by which we decide who we are and what we want to make of our lives. Our dream, then, contains the quality of a vision, an imagined possibility for ourselves in the world that generates

WEAVING FAITH AND EXPERIENCE

excitement and a zest for life. In religious language, our dream is our vocation. Since Vatican II, the Catholic understanding of vocation has undergone a dramatic transformation. In the piety of past generations which many of us remember, to "have a vocation" meant to be a vowed religious or priest. The rest of us, married or single, carried on without any special religious identity or sense of calling.

Today, a more adequate theology of baptism insists that every Christian has a vocation to holiness and to mission. By holiness we mean our personal response to God's invitation to love God with our whole being and love our neighbor as ourselves. By mission, we refer to God's invitation to devote our gifts and talents to a particular way of loving, working, and contributing to the realization of God's kingdom in the world.

Levinson's research suggests that women who build a life structure around a dream in early adulthood have a better chance to find personal meaning and fulfillment. Women who betray their dream in their twenties will have to deal later with the consequences. Those without a dream of their own, who piggyback on someone else's, will inevitably drift into an early life structure with no particular sense of self in the world. Other young women are not yet clear enough about who they are and what they want to do with their lives to pursue a definite path. Levinson explores the various choices young women made as they entered into the unfamiliar terrain of adulthood. Let us reflect upon those choices as a way of gaining insight into our own.

The Relational Dream
This dream refers to forming relationships, most typically, though not always, through marriage and motherhood. Ideally, a woman seeks a relationship with a special man and builds a life around him. Her dream is to become a certain kind of wife and mother. Many of the women who participated in Levinson's study freely chose the relational dream. They met someone with whom they thought they could fulfill their dream of becoming a wife and mother. A woman in her late six-

ties reflects back on her decision to marry in her twenties:

> As graduation approached I had absolutely no ambition. I knew I
> wasn't ready for marriage, but if you weren't married and didn't have
> kids by twenty-one you were an old maid. I always was a good girl
> and did what was expected. I got married at twenty and got pregnant
> on the honeymoon.[3]

Levinson suggests that most of us think of marriage as an emotional
relationship between the partners. In fact, the data suggests that marriage is never simply about being in love. It is, first of all, about build-
ing an enterprise in which the partners can have a good life and meet
their goals and aspirations. The concept of "marriage enterprise" was
one of the major fruits of Levinson's research. One twenty-two-year-
old woman writes,

> I didn't fall in love with him but I liked him very much. He was nice
> to be with and didn't put any demands on me sexually. He was a
> really decent guy. I liked his family very much, and my family liked
> him. Our families and backgrounds were similar. I thought I could
> have a nice life with him.[4]

The Career Dream

This dream refers to becoming a certain kind of individual through
forming a career identity such as becoming a news anchor, actress, psychologist, rock singer, nurse, dental hygienist, teacher, lawyer or scien-
tist, or forming a religious identity by joining a religious congregation.
World War II and the women's movement of the twentieth century
made it more acceptable for women to pursue a career path. Levinson
identifies these women as attempting to actualize what he refers to as
the "internal anti-traditional figure" rather than the "internal traditional
homemaker figure."[5]

Levinson's description of the struggle between these two internalized images in the life stories of women he interviewed has helped

many women makes sense out of their own experience. The "internal traditional homemaker figure" refers to the societal expectation of women to marry, raise a family, and continue the basic traditions of the family of origin. The "internal anti-traditional figure" refers to a woman's investment in a career that could equal or outweigh her investment in family. These two terms provide the language for many women to name and better understand the ongoing tension, struggle, and at times "mortal combat" they describe as they forge a truce between these two dimensions of their lives. One woman writes,

> Is it possible to liberate myself from the narrow constraints of the traditional pattern? Can I participate in family life without being a traditional homemaker? Can I participate in the male work world with inner commitment and equality? How can I have a career without jeopardizing my femininity and my involvement in family?[6]

Women Without a Dream

This category refers to young women who do not have a dream. Some can't identify anything or anyone that gives them a sense of direction, excitement, or purpose; others drift into a job or a marriage without sufficient reflection as to its suitability as a valid expression of themselves; still others have a basic sense of being overwhelmed, of having no way to form a minimally good enough life as an adult. For some, the crisis involved considerable turmoil and conscious suffering, while others were not clearly aware of the extent of their difficulties. One young woman in her early thirties reflects,

> I look back on those years and it seems amazing. Where was I? I never questioned anything then. I just meandered through all those years without ever thinking about anything. It was like I lived in a fog…. The image that comes to my mind of my twenties is like a cocoon. I sat by myself most of the time just kind of wrapped and cushioned against the real world. I sat there and waited for something to happen. I could have sat there a long time.[7]

Relational and Career Dreams

A fourth group of young women chose to balance relational and career dreams at the same time. These women wanted occupations which fulfilled them as individuals. They also wanted to combine career with the relational dream of marriage and family. Twenty years ago, these women were on the cutting edge, carving out a new option for women. Today, many women presume the right to integrate both. A twenty-seven-year-old woman comments,

> I recently married, so I feel quite happy with the relational aspects of my life, but I would also like to have a career before we start a family. I'm still searching for my niche in that area, starting my second master's degree at twenty-seven.[8]

The essential task, then, for the spring of life is forming and giving shape to one's dream—one's sense of self in the adult world. Often it is provisional at best. Yet, the form that the dream takes or doesn't provides the first framework for entering the adult world. As we look back on the springtime of our lives from the perspective of our middle years, the following questions emerge: What choices did we make? Did we have a dream? If so, did we choose marriage and family life? Or, were we drawn to pursue a particular career or religious life? How did the choices we made influence our subsequent development and where we are today? Most importantly, was God involved in our lives and the choices we made, or was God a dim, distant figure?

To gain insight into the interweaving of the human and spiritual journey during the springtime of our lives, let us explore what kind of spiritual growth might take place as we live though the consequences of the choices we made.

Interpersonal Faith

God comes to us in our history. What invitations did God extend to us during the springtime of our lives? There is a world of difference between knowing *about* someone and actually *knowing* them. In the spring of our lives, our ability to fall in love on a human level often functions as a moment of grace (*kairos*) on a spiritual level. It involves "waking up" to the discovery of God as *personal* in a way that is possible only when we have grown into the capacity to fall in love with another. In other words, it is the experience of *passionate* romantic love in our human experience that foreshadows what falling in love with God can be like. We become capable of experiencing God as a divinely *personal* Other—friend, lover, companion—who invites us into a personal relationship.

In the Old Testament literature, the Song of Solomon expresses this experience. Through imagery that is romantic and sensual, it tells a story about a lover in search of her beloved.

> My beloved speaks and says to me:
> "Arise, my love, my fair one,
>   and come away;
> for now the winter is past,
>   the rain is over and gone.
> The flowers appear on the earth;
>   the time of singing has come,
> and the voice of the turtledove
>   is heard in our land... (Song of Solomon 2:10–12)

A long line of Christian mystical writers such as Gregory of Nyssa, Bernard of Clairvaux, Mechthild of Magdeburg, Teresa of Avila, and John of the Cross have been inspired by this text and celebrate it as expressing the love between Christ and the individual soul. In the New Testament, the stories of discipleship are not initially stories about mission, but about a relationship with Jesus. The disciples became attached to the person of Jesus to such an extent that they gradually came to share his vision of life and ministry.

> The next day John again was standing with two of his disciples, and
> as he watched Jesus walk by, he exclaimed, "Look, here is the Lamb

of God!" The two disciples heard him say this, and they followed Jesus. When Jesus turned and saw them following, he said to them, "What are you looking for?" They said to him, "Rabbi" (which translated means Teacher), "where are you staying?" He said to them, "Come and see." They came and saw where he was staying, and they remained with him that day. (John 1:35–39)

This scriptural passage illustrates Jesus' invitation to personal relationship: "Come and see." That is, come and get to know me, my mind and heart. And give me the opportunity to know you. The following descriptions of faith as the discovery of a personal relationship with God illustrate the spiritual awakening that can take place at this time.

As I began to gain more perspective on myself and my relationship with men, so also could I begin to detect a new sort of hunger emerging for exploring more deeply my relationship with God. It was as if, through this crisis of whether or not to break up with my boyfriend, I had discovered a new, more personal and compassionate God—in many ways a God far different from the distant and demanding father God of my childhood.[9]

My spirituality is starting to grow rapidly. Growing up as a Catholic, I tended to go through the motions, but now I am starting to learn more and more about my faith and my relationship with God. With my faith growing I am finding myself to be a more spiritual person. My spiritual journey is never ending and always widening.[10]

These personal testimonies of a growing love relationship with God in the springtime of life suggest *possibilities*, not *actualities*. There are a variety of faith responses that can occur at this time. Some young adults continue to live the "faith of the clan." What was good enough for Mom and Dad is good enough for me. For many others, however, adolescence and young adulthood initiate a restless time of questioning, and often, a time of drifting away from their religious faith.

In a fascinating study of young adults appropriately titled, *Googling God: The Religious Landscape of People in their 20s and 30s,* Mike Hayes shares the results of his research on the faith stance of young adults.[11] He points out that for the most part, the richly textured Catholic subculture that many of us grew up with, which shaped and helped sustain Catholic spirituality in the past, has disappeared. Most young adults today have not known an integrated Catholic world which transmits a coherent vision of faith. Rather, they have gleaned fragments of their spirituality from various sources including families, parish liturgies, youth retreats, religious education classes, popular media, and for some, Catholic schools. This process has produced young adults with greater tolerance for religious pluralism but less institutional loyalty. Many of us who grew up with the institutional church as the centerpiece of our faith may be disturbed by this lack of communal affiliation.

Hayes explores the diversity of young adult faith by distinguishing seven types of spirituality. These categories are not the only way to describe young adults' spiritual search, but they are helpful for gaining insight into the diversity of faith expressions at this time of their lives. Not surprising, many middle-aged adults find these descriptions helpful as they seek to better understand the choices of their adult children, their friends, as well as some of their own faith struggles.

Eclipsed: These young adults show no interest in spirituality or religious matters. They have better things to do. They do not attend Mass and seldom pray. Some feel they are too busy or have higher priorities, while others experience guilt feelings about not being more involved in their faith. Yet they remain religious beings and identify themselves as Catholic in surveys. Their spirituality has not died, but has been eclipsed by their current concerns.

Private: These young adults seldom attend liturgies or participate in church activities. They find little use for outward display of public ritual, pursuing spiritual goals in other ways. For example, they read religious books, find God in nature, attend yoga classes to center and calm themselves, pray privately while jogging, driving, or walking the beach.

Ecumenical: A growing number of young adults simply assume that the divisions among Christians make no sense, and that we all should unite and work together. Some are faithful to their Catholic heritage, but others have little institutional loyalty. They have no problem joining another Christian denomination if they feel it will bring them closer to Christ and serve their spiritual needs.

Evangelical: This group refers to young adults who speak easily about their personal relationship with Jesus and are attracted to prayer groups with high emotional energy. Some belong to charismatic prayer groups and many enjoy a style of liturgy that is vibrant and emotive. Normally they are enthusiastic and involved in their faith.

Sacramental: Many young adults love their church and find their spiritual nourishment through fairly regular participation in the official liturgy and traditional practices. The sacraments provide the context within which they meet the Lord working in their lives. Many have a sense of the sacramental nature of the world, seeing the spirit of God in all things.

Prophetic: Many parishes and campus ministry programs have groups of young adults committed to working in various ways for justice and peace in the world. They align themselves with the goals of organizations like Men and Women for Others, Pax Christi, and Bread for the World. They devote themselves to causes such as racial harmony, environmental health, and serving the poorest of the poor.

Communal: Many young adults yearn for, but often cannot find, a group of people who share their beliefs and values. When they do, they delight in worshiping with kindred spirits at Mass. They make retreats and/or join faith sharing groups.

As we see, there are a variety of faith stances among young adults today. Furthermore, there is considerable overlapping—a young adult can be involved in more than one faith stance at a time. As I noted earlier, these styles of faith help to explain some of the choices of middle-aged adults as well. One woman in her fifties, who loves her Catholic faith, comments that her greatest challenge is, "keeping my college-age children in touch with God and their Church."[12] But another woman states, "I have come to the realization that the Roman Catholic Church is dead in relation to life in the United States. I am looking elsewhere."[13] Finally, a woman in her seventies notes, "I'm searching. I am working on praying; how to find God in other places— through other sources like Buddhism, other avenues of learning, the spiritualities of other people and their way to God. I'm encouraged to have the opportunity to learn more about the Path."[14]

As we look back at the springtime of our lives, what was our faith experience? Did we equate faith solely with knowing *about* God through codes, creeds, and rituals, or did we also "wake up" to an experience of God inviting us into a deep personal relationship? Did we drift into a style of life that excluded God or kept God at a compartmentalized distance? However we describe the interweaving of our faith and human experience through the choices we made or didn't make, the story of Jeremiah and the potter is instructive. Whether we were aware of it or not, God continued to work with us, molding us and forming us into the young women both we and God desired us to become. It is always a collaborative effort. God respects our freedom too much to force any response from us. Yet God is always encouraging us to make the choices that bring us to greater freedom and love. "I came that they may have life, and have it abundantly" (John 10:10).

The Summer of Life

The springtime of life gradually gives way to the season of summer. The issues and tasks of the summer of a woman's life, ages twenty-eight to thirty-nine, are contingent upon her satisfaction with the choices made and the life lived during her twenties. As you may recall from the introduction, Levinson makes a distinction within each season between *stable* periods within which we live out decisions we have made, and *tran-*

sitional periods when we question whether we want to change or modify our choices so as to enrich our lives and further our dreams.

No matter how satisfied we may be with the choices made thus far, it is impossible for a young woman to fulfill all her dreams for every arena of her life in the springtime of her life. Consequently, women approaching age thirty, recognizing that the decade of the twenties will soon be over, often find themselves asking: What do I really want from life? What do I give to, and receive from, my marriage, family, work, friends, church? What do I need to change in myself, and in my situation, so that I can have a better life?

For women who chose marriage and family life in their twenties and who are happy with their choice, the age thirty transition is barely noticeable. For women who are dissatisfied with their choice, this is the time for reassessment. What needs to be done to enrich family life? Can I stay in this marriage? Do we now want to have children? Do we desire more children?

For women who chose the career dream, the often harsh reality of what it takes to make it in the world of work brings on a time of reappraisal. Levinson's study of women pursuing careers noted,

> Many career women went through a marked, often painful process as they became aware of the competitive struggles, the "politics" of organizational life, and the diverse obstacles to advancement for women. The work world was not as caring nor as rational as the young women had expected, and the career women's progress within it depended upon much more than their own ability and experience. The career women had to reappraise their occupational aspirations and the relative value they placed on work, family and other aspects of life.[15]

For career women who were also single, the internal pressure to stabilize their lives through marriage and family became paramount. Research data suggests that at this time of reassessment, women must come to terms with the issue of marriage and parenting in both a quantitatively and qualitatively different way than is the case for men. Even though today more women put off having children until later, reaching the age of thirty-five raises the following questions: Will I ever marry and have children? If not, can I be happy and fulfilled as a career woman? What can I do to make relationships more central in my life? Who are the friends, coworkers, siblings, and extended family members who make up a network of support and care for me? How do I sustain and nurture those relationships? For the women who endeavored to integrate marriage, family, and career, the age thirty transition is a time to reassess the quality and progression of both their dreams and their ability to achieve a balance between the two.

As we journey down memory lane from the perspective of our middle years to the decade of our thirties, what do we find? Were we satisfied with the consequences of our choices or were we disappointed, looking to make significant changes? If we were basically satisfied with our lives, were there opportunities to give our lives more meaning and value? A woman religious writes, "The challenge of this stage of my life was to let go of the fantasies I had about religious life and the church and integrate the reality that even the world of religion is composed of both darkness and light."[16] A married woman notes, "I face the challenge of balancing family, work and aging parents. My children are at an impressionable age, and I want to be a good role model."[17] A single woman sighs, "I'm getting bored with my career. I want to move on to the next stage of my life; that is, kids, marriage, family. I want more meaningful friendships with other religious people. I'm thinking about my parents all the time—healing painful memories."[18]

This last vignette reminds many of us that conflict and anxieties originating in childhood often continue to plague us as adults. The transition to age thirty provides a second chance to deal with unresolved issues of childhood and the twenties and to form a life structure appropriate for the thirties.

Reflective Faith

There is an old cultural assumption, largely unexamined by the human sciences, that by age twenty or so, people normally establish a life structure that will continue unchanged throughout the adult years. While that assumption may have been true for generations past, it is no longer true for adults today. Many young adults explore a variety of options before settling into a career or marriage. High school and college students now are told by vocational counselors that they can expect to change jobs or careers many times in their lives.

Yet, as women and men move into the decade of their thirties, they tend to become more serious about who they want to be and what they want to do with their lives. This growing up, or growing "down" more deeply into the meaning and purpose of life, describes the faith response of many young women. I have named it "reflective faith."

Reflection is the act of deliberately slowing down our normal processes of making sense of our lives to take a closer look at our experience and at our framework for interpretation. We reflect when something happens to us that we cannot easily fit into the categories we normally use to make meaning in our lives. So, whether we have a strong faith life or whether we have put God on the back burner so to speak, there are often experiences at this time in our lives which propel us to own or reject religious faith as "*my* faith."

This awakening can happen though a single event or can occur over a period of time. Each person's experience is unique. It may stem from times of difficulty and crisis: a decision over birth control or abortion, illness, divorce, the death of a parent, spouse, or child. It can be brought on by the experience of personal harassment, oppression, financial problems, or discrimination in the workplace or church. Such experiences serve to bring the question of meaning, and therefore, the question of God to the conscious surface of our life: Where is God in my life? Who really is God for me? One woman writes,

Steve and I stopped going to church when I was thirty-three, mainly on my initiative. With my parents' split and my father's death and dealing with my mother, I just couldn't take it anymore. I got a new attitude toward religion. It was about God taking care of you. I realized that, in the final analysis, you have to take care of yourself. It took me a long time to grow up.[19]

On the other hand, the awakening can happen through positive life experiences such as falling in love, giving birth to a child, the loyalty of friends, the stability of marriage, the rewards of a meaningful job—experiences which put us in touch with the sacred dimension of life. One woman writes:

I felt godlike—a miracle worker. It was the best moment of my life. I felt my baby's head, then saw his face—I got to cut his cord and put him to my breast. I felt like I did the impossible. I couldn't believe he was finally out into the light. I felt holy.[20]

The sacred dimension of life is also experienced by women who feel close to God and want to grow in holiness through each new phase of their lives. One thirty-two-year-old woman writes,

I've fallen head over heels in love with a God who is head over heels in love with me. I call him, "My Lord, My God, My Beloved." I have a very strong relationship with the Lord. He is with me always and I connect with him throughout the day. I hope to grow in holiness especially as I prepare for marriage and family in the next year or two.[21]

The particular challenge of these years is to explore more deeply how God invites us to grow in holiness through the concrete circumstances of our lives. In my work with women, I find there are three areas, in particular, that women experience at this stage of their lives as either blocks or avenues to God's grace: sexuality, family life, and work.

Sexuality

Many of us grew up with a negative view of sexuality. Sexuality was equated with "having sex." It was not talked about in many Christian homes. At best, sexuality was tolerated as necessary to fulfill the procreative end of marriage; at worst it was "dirty," and viewed with deep suspicion as the chief source and vehicle of sin.

This attitude toward sexuality, evident in the writing of some theologians, was influenced by a dualistic philosophy which taught that to reach God we had to leave our world, our bodies, our sexuality behind and ascend to God who is spirit. A "spirit=good/body=bad" dichotomy emerged and a distorted view of sexuality ensued. Spirit came to be understood as the eternal and good part of the self, while body came to be understood as the mortal, temporal, and sinful part of the self.

Today theologians speak of sexuality in much broader, healthier terms. Rather than equating sexuality with "having sex," they maintain that sexuality refers to the desire for intimacy and communion physically, emotionally, and spiritually with others and with God. One woman from Levinson's study shares her personal experience of growing into a broader notion of sexuality:

> I understand now that sex isn't just physical; it is a relationship that is connected to the way the two people fit into each other's life. I've always felt that I had to be in control of everything or I was in danger. In this relationship I've had no control and it is okay. I can just be myself. There is mutuality in our feelings for each other; we can be together without saying a word. He is part of me as a person, blending in with my needs and interest in a totality of things. I never had that experience before, and it is a time in my life, finally, when I am ready for that.[22]

Sexuality involves the recognition and experience of our incompleteness and separateness that drives us toward love, communion, family, friendship, wholeness, and holiness. In other words, the very energy that draws us into relationship with others is the same energy that draws us into relationship with God. Sexuality, then, lies at the center of our spiritual life.

This understanding of sexuality encourages us to take a second look at the meaning of *eros*. In contemporary usage, *eros* refers to the *erotic*. It often conjures up images of pornography, lust, and seedy adult bookstores. Yet, the classical meaning of *eros* is broader and, in the best sense, earthy. It refers to the sensual face of love, to our passions and our passionate drive for life and growth. Most importantly, it refers quite literally to being in touch. Such experiences as arousal and affection, passion and response, intimacy and appreciation are all part of *eros*. As such, they are avenues of God's grace.

As we know too well, *eros* has its dark side. When it turns in on itself in the pursuit of pleasure as an end in itself, it becomes possessive, controlling, and manipulative. Thus *eros* has to be integrated with *agape*—the ability to put the needs of others above our own.

Yet, *agape*, when disconnected from the energy and motivation of *eros*, can become mere obligation and duty. Some women appear to be good Christians in that they do all the right things. Yet there doesn't seem to be any passion, vitality, or conviction about what they do. *Eros* and *agape* need each other. When they are united, they lead to true, self-giving love of others and of God.

One of the challenges of our times is to reunite sexuality and spirituality. We grow in wholeness and holiness *in* and *through* our sexuality. Our attitude toward sexuality can be a block or an avenue of God's grace. Which has it been for us?

Family Life

How do we view family life? Do we see it as an avenue of God's grace or as a distraction? A woman in her thirties with young children writes,

> Because of the strain of raising small children, I can't be as spiritual
> or as close to God as I want to be for myself, for my husband, and for
> my children. I pray in the car, in the shower, and especially at 3 AM

(Dear God, please make her sleep!), but not in the contemplative way
I feel would make me closer to God.[23]

While this woman rightfully longs for quiet time to nurture her relationship with God, she also needs to realize that being attentive to
God's presence in her children and all the people and activities that
make up her day is a form of contemplation as well. For too long in the
church the laity has been schooled in a monastic spirituality which told
us that we had to leave the world to find God. The Second Vatican
Council changed all that by embracing an incarnational spirituality that
reminds us that everything is grace. Consequently, the true contemplative in action is one who knows that everything she does—changing
diapers, washing dishes, cleaning the house, creating a delicious meal,
dealing with a difficult teenager, or a husband out of work—is not a distraction, but on the contrary, if done out of love and for the glory of
God, brings us into a deeper union with God, even when, and especially
when, we don't feel it. One woman writes:

> My faith has always been to find God in everything I do—being a
> mom of young children and teenagers; spending time with each set
> of parents [hers and her husband's]; helping to support my family
> financially. I have nothing left over at the end of the day. Yet I am
> peaceful knowing that all I have done has been out of love for them
> and for God.[24]

Our model for the integration of prayer and action in our lives is Jesus.
Mark's Gospel describes a typical day in his life (Mark 1.21-30). Jesus
spends his day teaching and healing in the synagogue. Then, with
James and John, he goes to the home of Simon and Andrew, undoubtedly looking for food and relaxation. Simon's mother-in-law had gone
to bed with fever; Jesus heals her and she began to wait on them. After
dinner, townsfolk brought to him all who were sick and possessed by
devils. And he cured many who were suffering from one disease or
another. Then, early the next morning, long before dawn, Jesus left the

house and went off to a lonely place to pray. It is worth noting that the majority of his day was spent serving people. He prayed at the end of a very busy day and evening, or before another day's work began. This was his time for communing with his God and discerning the next step in his ministry. His day was much like our own; we should receive encouragement from it.

Jesus models for us a unity between love of God and love of neighbor that should be the hallmark of our lives as well. Our time of prayer enables us to put on the mind and heart of Jesus *so that* we learn to recognize him in the faces and activities of our day. One woman in her mid-thirties writes,

> As a busy mother of three children under ten years of age I must admit that I have long abandoned all hope of setting rigid schedules for prayer and Scripture reading. I have learned that a busy woman's basic strategy is to make the most of opportunities that come my way. I now watch for the "lulls" and sandwich my prayer between school bells and trips to the store for peanut butter and jelly. I know from experience that these are the moments that keep me aware that God is present, active and first in my daily living, even when I am doing three things at once.[25]

All of us, then, need to find a rhythm between our daily activities and our personal prayer, remembering that God is found in both. Mother Teresa of Calcutta, a woman who found God in every person she met, reminds us that God often comes to us in the distressing disguise of family life.

> It is easy to smile at people outside your own home. It is so easy to take care of the people that you don't know well. It is difficult to be thoughtful, and kind, and to smile and be loving to your own in the house day after day, especially when we are tired and in a bad temper or bad mood. We all have these moments and that is the time that Christ comes to us in a distressing disguise.[26]

Work

For many of us the most difficult place to find God is in our work. Can it truly be an avenue of God's grace? While our spirituality can be personal, it cannot be private. As disciples of Jesus, all of us are called to bring gospel values of peace, justice, and love not only into our homes, but also into the workplace.

In their Pastoral Letter on Stewardship, the Catholic bishops warn that today there is a strong tendency to privatize faith, to push it to the margins of society, confining it to people's hearts, or at best, their homes, while excluding it from the marketplace where men and women acquire a view of life and its meaning—a view that often contradicts the values of the gospel. They challenge us to give generously of our time, talent, and treasure according to the gifts and talents we have received so that we can partner with God in the transformation of society.[27]

Women now have opportunities in the workplace that were unavailable to our mothers and grandmothers. Yet we enter the workforce with mixed motivation. Many women work out of necessity. Others have gifts and talents that they want to express through a particular profession. Some find the workplace interesting and creative; others find the workplace dehumanizing and oppressive. Whatever our particular motivation for entering the workplace, it provides women with a significant challenge: Can we view our jobs as an opportunity to exercise a ministry of presence and witness to the Christian values of compassion, justice, concern for people, and charity toward all? A quote attributed to Francis of Assisi is applicable here: "Preach the gospel always. When necessary use words." One woman writes,

> As a manager at Barnes and Noble, I try to be the presence of Christ to all who seek my help. I give each person my full attention. I help them find whatever they are looking for. I am amazed by the life stories I hear and the support I am able to give just by listening.[28]

Many women have spoken to me about the sense of meaning they receive when they view their work as ministry. They describe going about their normal activities with the intention of serving God through the people and tasks of their day. Such work includes cleaning homes, sales at a local department store, nursing on an oncology floor, selling real estate, teaching mathematics, searching for a cure for cancer, directing development of a large hospital, practicing law for abused women and their children.

Yet, others have described work as drudgery, as a source of stress and a drain on their energy, something they resent and do not look forward to. Yet if that work, as difficult as it is, is undertaken for the honor and glory of God—God will bless it and bring some kind of good out of it.

What has been the role of work in our lives? Did we work because we had to or because we felt we had something to contribute to a particular enterprise? Has it been a source of meaning and purpose for us, or has it been something we had to do to pay the bills and put food on the table? Did we experience it as an obstacle to our spiritual growth or as a means to love God through serving others?

So much of how we view our work—or almost anything in life— depends upon the attitude we bring to it. I find myself challenged by the attitude of a young Jewish woman, Etty Hillesum, who, during World War II, could have escaped the concentration camp at Westerbork, but instead freely chose to accompany many of her people there and eventually to Auschwitz where she died. Many of the letters that made it out of the camp bear testimony to her determination to find beauty in the midst of misery; to find God in the unspeakable suffering of her people. Her prayer can be an incentive for us to find God in all things as well, "My life has become an uninterrupted dialogue with you, O my God."[29]

As we look back over the decade of our thirties, what does the interweaving of the human and spiritual journey of our lives look like? Many of us settled into, and gave fruitful expression to, the dreams and choices of our twenties. Others of us reevaluated and modified those choices to provide a richer meaning and direction for our lives. Still others experienced disappointment and heartache as we endured separation, divorce, physical or mental abuse, financial setbacks, and other experiences that thwarted our dreams and called into question the possibility of finding real happiness and meaning in our lives.

As we claimed more ownership of our lives, so, too, many of us claimed more ownership of our faith as we grappled with the question: Who really is God *for me?* For many of us it was a time of deepening our relationship with God, and growing in our ability, through grace, to find God in the circumstances of our lives. For others it was a time to reevaluate and reject an image of God and a view of our faith which blocked our ability to find God in our sexuality, our family life, and our work. For still others, it was a time when God didn't figure much into our lives at all.

We began this chapter by suggesting that we do not enter the middle years with a "clean slate," so to speak, but as women formed by the dreams we pursued, the choices we made, the successes we celebrated, and the wounds we endured during the spring and summer of our lives. These seasons of our lives, for better or worse, form the backdrop that sets the stage for the next season, the autumn of our lives. These years from forty to sixty-five are described as the middle years. They form the heart of this book. It is to those years we now turn. Whoever we have become, whether we are ready or not, we now enter the autumn of life.

FOOD FOR THOUGHT

1. As you look back over the spring and summer of your life, what memories come to mind? Did you have a dream, a sense of yourself in the world? If you had a dream, did you think of it as a vocation, as your particular way of serving God and growing in holiness?
2. As you reflect upon these seasons of life, can you identify specific instances where God was guiding you, even though you may not have recognized it at the time? How did you view sexuality, family life,

work? Did you consider them as blocks or avenues of God's grace? How do you view them now?

3. I used the terms "Faith as Personal Relationship" and "Faith as Reflective Faith" to describe the texture of our faith during the spring and summer of life. Do these terms resonate with your experience, or are there others that better fit your faith at this point in your life?

REFLECTION

"Open"
with a flick of a wrist
and one quick turn, the sign now read:
"Closed."

We've seen the sign
on business doors,
libraries,
even churches.
Public facilities have their days and seasons
of availability and closure.

As God walks the universe
and encounters human souls,
a sign hangs at the entrance
of every mind, of every heart.

Is it "Open" or "Closed"?

The Lord awaits our decision.[30]

—Robert Morneau

PRAYER

Where you are (however unchosen) is the place of blessing.
How you are (however broken) is the place of grace.
Who you are, in your becoming, is your place in the kingdom.[31]

—Margaret Silf

Dear Lord,
As long as you are with me in
the Where,
the How
and the Who
of my life,
I know I will find my way
home to You.
For You are both my path
and my compass.

CHAPTER TWO

• THE AUTUMN OF LIFE: PARADOXICAL FAITH •

In the middle of the journey of our life
I came to myself within a dark wood
Where the straight way was lost.[1]
—Dante

For those of us who live in the Midwest, there is nothing like an Indian summer day in autumn. The weather is unseasonably warm; the air is brisk; the leaves on the trees reach their peak—brilliant shades of orange, yellow, and red. People enjoy football games and tailgate parties, cider mills and apples, Halloween trick-or-treating, and Thanksgiving gatherings. Yet, in the midst of anticipating and enjoying this season, we now and again feel a twinge of sadness. Winter is right around the corner.

Autumn is the transitional season between the growth and blossoming of spring, the full bloom of summer and the darkness and death of winter. Such rhythms characterize the autumn of our lives as well—the "middle years" that span the decades of our forties and fifties.

Morning and Afternoon of Life

Many of us begin our forties feeling that we are at the peak of our lives physically, mentally, and spiritually. Yet sometime between the late thirties and mid-forties, it dawns on us that nearly half our life is over. This realization leads to what twentieth-century psychiatrist Carl Jung described as the midlife crisis. Jung made a distinction between the morning and afternoon of life. Each has its own unique challenges and tasks. The morning of life—seasons of spring and summer—is oriented primarily to our relationship with the *outer* world: Who am I? What do I want to do with my life? What career will I pursue? How am I viewed by others? What steps should I take to be a successful wife, mother, religious, or career woman?

The afternoon of life is oriented primarily to attending to our relationship with our *inner* world: Who have I become? Where am I going in life? What do I really want? What legacy do I want to leave behind? Both the morning and afternoon of life have their part to play in what Jung identified as the process of individuation; that is, becoming a unique individual, our true self. Jung stressed the significance of the second half of life when neglected, repressed, or unattended dimensions of our personalities—"voices from the other rooms"— begin to clamor for attention and integration. He cautioned women and men to listen to the neglected voices of the inner self and make the changes necessary to integrate these dimensions of the personality into our conscious lives. Unfortunately, Jung maintained that most adults are ill-prepared for the challenge of individuation.

> The worst of it all is that intelligent and cultivated people live their lives without even knowing the possibility of such transformation. Wholly unprepared, they embark upon the second half of life. Are there perhaps colleges for forty-year olds to prepare them for their coming life? No, thoroughly unprepared we take the step into the afternoon of life with the false assumption that our truths and ideals will serve us. But we cannot live the afternoon of life according to the program of life's morning; for what was great in the morning will be little at evening, and what in the morning was still true at evening will have become a lie.... I have given psychological treatment to too many people of advancing years, and have looked often into the secret chambers of their souls not to be moved by this fundamental truth.[2]

Jung explained the midlife experience through the image of a mountain. While climbing up the mountain we have all the time in the world. If we choose the wrong path we still have time to change course and continue our ascent. However, once we reach the top, the horizon changes from "there is still so much time ahead," to "how much time do I have left?" Age forty signals the midway mark. What do we have to show for it? Time to make changes is limited. This critical transition invites us to bring the first half of our life to a close, and make adjustments for a fruitful second half.

Midlife Issues

In his study of the life stories of men and women, Levinson never set out with a preconceived notion of tracking a midlife transition. He states, "We did not begin with the hypothesis of a highly defined transition at midlife. It emerged in the course of our research."[3] Data confirmed that the midlife transition occurred between the ages of thirty-eight to forty-five. Levinson cautions that not every woman experiences midlife in the same way with the same intensity or with the same concerns. Yet, he discovered similar themes in the life experiences of many women.

The first theme summons women and men to turn inward. One woman in her early forties describes this movement from an outward to an inward orientation.

> It's a funny switch. You measure yourself by very external things for a long time and then a switch takes place. You recognize that you're going to judge yourself and your happiness and your fulfillment by internal feelings, not by where you are on any ladder. It's the inner goal that I'm running against now.[4]

The experience of aging and facing our mortality are the motivating factors of the inward turn. Levinson notes that beyond the concern with personal survival, there is a concern about meaning. It is bad enough to feel that our lives will soon be over. It is even worse if we feel that our lives have not had—and may never have—sufficient value for ourselves and the world. Concern about our life's meaning and value usually inaugurates a process of reassessment: What have I done with my life thus far? What do I want to make of it in the future?

A second theme that emerged for women is how to grow older gracefully in a culture that glorifies youth. Women begin to grieve the passing of their youth in a variety of ways. Some try to reclaim it. The millions of dollars spent on facial and body creams that promise a restored youth illustrate the often desperate search for a remedy to the aging process. The principal of an affluent Catholic girls' high school once remarked that when she stands in front of a group of mothers and daughters, she often is not sure who the mothers are and who the daughters are! Other women begin to gain weight and seem to lose interest in their appearance. Most women, however, find ways to age gracefully through good hygiene, regular exercise, a balanced diet, and intentional cultivation of those qualities that get better with age—intelligence, competence, and wisdom.

Besides the inward turn and concerns about the aging process, a third theme to emerge for women in the decade of the forties is becoming our own person. In his conversations with women, Levinson noted that they often spoke about the wish "to be my own person" or "to be treated as a real person."

A woman growing into mature adulthood desires to be affirmed in her world—whatever that world is—to speak more with her own voice; to be recognized in her own right not merely as an appendage to her husband, children, parents, or boss. She wants to be, and to be viewed as, independent, competent, and responsible, and to be taken seriously in ways that distinguish adults from children. One woman recently told me about her decision to put her career on hold so that she could be a stay-at-home mom until her children finished grade school. Imagine her dismay when she overhead her eighth-grade son comment to a friend, "My mom is a parasite. She lives off my dad." This woman's experience is not meant to suggest that children of mothers who choose to stay home perceive their mothers in this way. But it does highlight the dilemma facing women who want to claim their own lives while also caring for the needs of others.

Women also desire to be affirmed not only for qualities long associated with the feminine—generosity, empathy, and compassion—but also for qualities associated with masculinity—ambition, leadership skills, and intellectual competence. An important goal for women in their forties and fifties is the integration of both sets of qualities within each person in the realization of the true self.

Many women agree with Eleanor Roosevelt's observation that the core issue for women in the second half of life is personal integrity.

> Somewhere along the line of development we discover what we really are and then we make our real decision for which we are responsible. Make that decision primarily for yourself because you can never really live anyone else's life, not even your own child's. The influence you exert is through your own life and what you become yourself.[5]

It is vital that women have a solid sense of self to bring *to* relationships rather than a fragile sense of self that continually changes depending upon what others want us to be or do for them. To find a balance between caring for self while also attending to the needs of others are two facets of the challenge women face in becoming their own persons.

The themes we have discussed thus far—the realization that half of our life is over; the inward turn that is brought about through facing the aging process as well as our mortality; the challenge of becoming our own person—these issues pose opportunities as well as challenges for women in their forties. How we choose to deal with them lead women either to a midlife *transition* or a midlife *crisis*.

Midlife Transition

A midlife *transition* functions as a bridge between early and middle adulthood. By age forty, give or take a few years, many women enter a time of inner questioning about the quality of their lives in relation to their earlier dreams. The distinguishing characteristic of the midlife transition is that the life structure we have in place—marriage, religious life, single life, career—remain intact as we consider minor or major modifications to accommodate the "voices from the other rooms,"—that is, those talents or goals we have not yet had the opportunity to realize.

For example, some women find themselves reappraising the married relationship by asking: "What is the nature of this marriage?" "What aspects of it do I want to modify or eliminate?" Many women describe themselves as very lucky to have met, married, and grown up with their best friend. These marriages continue to flourish with few bumps in the road. Other women face a variety of issues depending upon choices made in the first half life. Women who entered into a traditional marriage—a marriage in which a woman depended on her husband as provider and head of the household—may now seek a more egalitarian marriage based on a relationship of mutuality in love, intimacy, play, and work.

Other women come to terms with the strengths and limitations of their marriages and reaffirm their commitment. More than a few women acknowledge that if they knew then what they know now about themselves and their husbands, they would have chosen a different man to marry. However, they affirm their husbands as good men and recommit themselves to the marriage. For the increasing number of women who marry with both personal and professional goals, now is the time for a significant assessment regarding the quality of each. Finally, many women come to terms with the failure of their marriages through separation and/or divorce. They face the challenge of learning from this life passage so they can build a better future for themselves.

For those women who devoted the first half of their lives to marriage and family life, many now launch out into the public sphere where they can live out aspects of themselves that have formerly been dormant or suppressed. An Episcopalian woman recalls her decision to pursue a lifelong dream:

I was thirty-nine years old, washing dishes at the kitchen sink when it hit me—it's either now or never. Ever since I was a little girl I wanted to be a minister. I realized that if I didn't begin Divinity school soon, it would be too late. Within a few days I called my husband and teenage children together and told them my plan. They were not happy about it, but I'm determined to see it through. I believe I have the calling and the talent to be a good priest.[6]

Another similar experience involved the dream of becoming a lawyer:

I made myself a promise that I would be a stay-at-home mom while my daughters were young. I have never regretted that decision. I loved every minute of it. When my youngest daughter began a full day of school, I decided it was time to fulfill another dream of mine that I had put on the back burner—law school. I started part time at age forty-two. It took me longer than most, but I was able to balance both pretty well.[7]

Many women who chose a career path went through a reappraisal at this time and made changes to accommodate a shift in goals. For a religious sister who had dedicated several years of service in the missions, the midlife transition involved a return to the U.S. and a concerted effort to nurture friendships left behind and to build closer relationships with her extended family. For another woman, a promotion meant the fulfillment of her youthful dream:

At 40 I was promoted to regional director. The promotion meant having to move with my husband and family to Boston. The job was a tremendous success. It was a marvelous, beautiful satisfying fulfillment of a youthful dream.... It challenged me intellectually and made full use of my talents. On a personal level it was so much of what I'd always wanted that I'd never had before and may never have again. It was a fulfillment personally. I have never felt so good about myself before or since.[8]

For many women the modifications of midlife are simple, barely noticeable. Yet, they provide a sense of well-being and future inner growth for the women making them. Such modifications include a renewed interest in writing poetry, taking a pottery class, volunteering at a hospital, going back to school, starting a business, getting a real estate license, serving the poor at a soup kitchen, placing one's gifts at the service of a parish outreach committee. One young woman commented that she never knew her mother was such an accomplished pianist until she took it up again in her late forties. We don't have to look too far to realize that there are a myriad of ways that women, listening to the voices within, find opportunities to enrich their lives and become more fully themselves by developing gifts and talents that were neglected or forgotten as they sought other goals in the first half of life.

Midlife Crisis

While the midlife transition involves a modification of a woman's life structure, the midlife *crisis* occurs when the whole life structure a woman had built over the years is "up for grabs." A woman in her forties found out that after twenty-three years of marriage, her husband didn't want to be with her anymore:

> I was looking forward to having my companion to grow old with. After raising four children, I felt it was all downhill from now on. We could enjoy the profits of all those years of effort. Instead I found out my husband had a different agenda. My personal feeling is my husband didn't want to come face to face with his mortality. He didn't want to be a grandfather.[9]

For women who put off marriage and childbirth to pursue a career, reaching age forty without marriage and family life can be a devastating blow:

> When I graduated from college the choices seemed limitless. I wanted a chance to live independently for a few years but assumed

I'd still have the option to have children. But somehow by making that one choice so many years ago I've come down a path that year by year has led me farther and farther away from motherhood.

I turned 25, then 30, then 35, and the choices began to disappear. Now there's a strong probability that I'll never have a child. Not to have a child—ever—how is that possible? How did this happen to me?.... Will I come to mourn the loss of my unborn children? All I have in my life now is my work. What will happen when I don't have work or children—when there's nothing, a complete void in my life? It terrifies and saddens me. Being childless now feels like an all encompassing black hole.[10]

Other women come to peace with not having biological children. One woman speaks for many single women as well as married women without children when she writes, "I came to peace with not having birth children in my late thirties and never looked back. I married someone with children, but many women do not and are very fulfilled and 'holy' in their vocations."[11]

Thus far we have described women's experience of midlife and we have certainly seen that one size does not fit all! There are countless ways women approached and lived out the opportunities and challenges of the forties. For many it was a rich and rewarding time of life when they felt at their peak physically, mentally, and spiritually. For these women, midlife was a time to modify their life structure so as to deepen the meaning of their lives, accommodate new goals, or take steps toward achieving existing ones. For others, however, midlife was a time of crisis when everything they had built during the first half of their lives fell apart.

In his conversations with men and women about this time of their lives, Levinson coined two terms to describe the negative or disappointing experiences that many shared with him. "Disillusionment" involves the recognition that long-held assumptions and beliefs about the self and the world are not true. "Detribalization" refers to the critical assessment of those particular groups, institutions, and traditions that have the greatest significance in our lives. Let us take a look at some of the ways women talked about these experiences in their lives.

Disillusionment

Some women expressed disappointment with their marriages but did not have the courage to leave them. They felt that they had fulfilled their end of the bargain but received little of the care and love they were promised. Many became psychologically stuck, separated, or divorced. One woman in her middle forties describes her decision to stay in a less than satisfying marriage:

> My husband does not see me as I am, he just doesn't. We don't have much in common except the children. I've grown away from him, and that frightens me. I don't know if I'd have the courage to leave him because the other possibilities seem worse. A lot of women at work are living with husbands who are alcoholics, husbands who run out on them. Or else they're divorced and having a difficult time making it alone. We still have a good marriage, compared to lots of others. All in all my life is not bad as it is right now. It's stagnant but it's not bad.[12]

Other women, who married young, find themselves working through feelings of disappointment regarding their college or young adult children who seem neither to want much of a relationship with them once they leave home, nor to appreciate all that they received. Still other women express disappointment with the myth of the successful career; that is, they could have it all—career, marriage, family, leisure—everything, all at the same time. Many women around age forty found themselves coming to terms with the disparity between the dream and the reality. Some found themselves stuck at mid-level management with no opportunity to advance; others found that as they advanced the hours were longer, the problems greater, and the benefits less. Such experiences led women to reappraise and modify what Levinson referred to as the "tyranny of the dream." One woman writes,

I had some really bad bosses and no good ones. When I left the job it was because I had no more challenges and was bored. A good boss would have transferred me. Until recently, my bosses were intent on climbing themselves; they had no conception of nurturing people and giving them room to grow, especially a woman. There was always a privileged inner circle of young fair-haired sons who were allowed to advance.[13]

Detribalization

While some women dealt with the experience of disillusionment, others confronted what Levinson described as detribalization; that is, a reassessment of the role certain institutions played in their lives.

Some women were not only disappointed with, but became critical of the workplace when they experienced discrimination or sexism. One woman writes,

> Throughout my whole career and even now I was the only woman or one of a very few women in the job I was in.... When you're younger and you're discriminated against you keep wondering, "Maybe it's me. Maybe I'm inadequate." Now it just infuriates me.... I'm just sick after twenty years of fighting discrimination against women. As I have progressed in my profession and been very successful by any objective standard I am much more willing and ready to face up to discrimination when I come against it.[14]

The other institution that became a source of disappointment and subject of critique by many women is the church. The relationship of women to the Catholic church is a delicate and complicated issue. There are undoubtedly as many different responses to the church as there are women who consider themselves Catholic. However, for the sake of dealing with the issue of detribalization—that is, women taking a long hard look at the institutions that have formed them—I describe three stances of women.

First, many Catholic women hold the hierarchy of the church in high esteem. They are obedient, loyal, and would never think of disagreeing or calling into question any of the church's teaching. As one woman recently commented to me, "The bishops and priests are leaders in the church; our role is to be obedient and to serve them in whatever way we can."

There are other women who believe they are good Catholics even though they disagree with some of the church's teachings. Even on the hot button issues of women's ordination, birth control, abortion, and homosexuality, these women believe that being a faithful Catholic includes expressing their opinions as part of the *sensus fidelium* (the mind of the faithful). Many Catholic lay faithful believe that the Holy Spirit is within them as much as in the hierarchy of the church, and that they have the right and the responsibility to present their views in a respectful manner.[15]

Finally, there are women who feel betrayed by the church's teaching on women or feel they have been discriminated against by those in authority.

After completing a master's degree in theology and pastoral ministry, one woman shares her experience when applying for a position in parish ministry.

> Having been groomed for a position belonging to a friar I was devastated when the priest denied me the position because I was a woman. I entered a state of numbness.... It led me to question everything. Can I and can my daughter realize our vocation as baptized Christians within the tradition of the Catholic Church? [16]

For another woman, the hymn *Faith of our Fathers* elicited the following reaction: "I have heard that hymn a hundred times. But all of a sudden it hit me. What about the faith of *our mothers?*"[17]

Some women who became disillusioned with the church look to the writings of women theologians who identify themselves as Christian feminists for greater understanding of their struggle for equality within the church. The Christian feminist movement is dedicated to the realization of three goals: 1) The critique of any system or thought pattern that disparages the genuine humanity of women who are created in the image and likeness of God; 2) A retrieval of the life stories and writings of women who made valuable contributions to living the gospel in their particular historical setting, thereby becoming sources of inspiration for women today; 3) Writing theology and spirituality "with women's eyes"; that is, reflecting on our Christian faith from the perspective of women's experience, images, and life stories. For example, while all of us are aware that the Scriptures portray God as king, father, husband, lord, and master, many of us don't realize that the Scriptures also portray God as mother, midwife, baker woman, nurse, seamstress, and a woman in search of a lost coin. Recognizing the truth that insofar as God created both male and female in the divine image, God can be presented equally well by images of either has had very positive effects on women's sense of themselves as beloved by God.[18]

Whatever their reasons, many women in their forties find themselves questioning what the church really means to them, and what their relationship with the church will be in the future. Through their reassessment, many women acknowledge that even though the church, as with life, often does not measure up to their expectations, it is still *their* church. Such women recommit themselves to laboring with God to make the church a sacrament for God's healing presence in the world. Other women conclude that if they experience the church as uncommitted in word and deed to the equality and mutuality of women and men in all facets of life, they will go elsewhere.

As we look back on the decade of our forties, what stands out? Was this a time of personal satisfaction as we made positive strides in the fulfillment of our dreams and goals? Or, did we feel the "sands slipping away in the hourglass of our lives," as we found ourselves haunted by fears of aging and our mortality? Did we experience a midlife transition or crisis? How did it affect our future? Did we suffer through disillusionment when we realized that our life choices were based on truths that did not hold up through the strain of life? Or did we find ourselves subjecting institutions that formed us and upon which we relied to critique and reassessment as to their value in our future?

Such questions address the variety of midlife experiences. For many women it is disheartening to acknowledge that a marriage, profession, or ministry has not been as fulfilling as we had hoped. Even for those of us truly blessed with the fulfillment of our dreams in the morning of life, it is difficult to say good-bye to our youth and face the prospect of aging and death. Some of us fear our best years are behind us. As one religious sister expressed to me, "It is frightening to wake up at forty or fifty and suddenly realize that life is surely half over and where has the first half gone? After many years of service, was it worth it?" We find ourselves asking, "What now?" To answer that question, let us explore the paradoxical quality of adult Christian faith.

Paradoxical Faith

Throughout this book I have proposed that just as there are seasons to life, there are also seasons to faith. Faith is not just a noun; it is also a verb. It is not static but dynamic. There is a particular tone, quality, and texture to our faith response within each season of life. As I have listened to women tell their stories, I have chosen titles to describe what I have heard: *interpersonal faith* for the springtime of life; *reflective faith* for summer; and now, *paradoxical faith* for the autumn of our lives.

I chose the term *paradoxical* for I found that women, no matter how rich and meaningful these years may be, often speak about a twinge of sadness, if not at times real anxiety, about the fading of youth and the realization that half of life is over. For most women this sense of the fragility of life hits home in the decade of the forties; for others it is delayed into the fifties or sixties. Whenever the realization comes, through whatever circumstances of our lives—and it will—it raises the question: How do we continue to choose life, to create a vibrant future out of what feels at times like loss and decay?

In light of these concerns many of us instinctively realize that the faith that guided us through the first half of our lives isn't sufficient for the second half. One woman insightfully writes,

> The real crisis is not the turbulent period of adolescence, the depression, the midlife "crazies," but it is the will to move on, the will to leave behind the first half of one's life, which demands a whole new myth, story and meaning for the person to live out and understand.[19]

One of the most influential spiritual authors of our time, Thomas Merton, would agree. He cautions us that the spiritual journey is not about retraced steps. It is about venturing into new land, along paths that we never walked, marked only by the footprints of those who have gone before us, and lighted by the invitation to "come follow me."[20]

The Mystical Tradition

The mystics of our tradition are those great friends of God who have gone before us and light the way for us. The great twentieth-century theologian Karl Rahner claims that the Christian of the future will be a mystic—that is, a person who has experienced God—or nothing at all.

Many of us who grew up before Vatican II were not exposed to the mystics of our tradition. One woman religious, looking back on those years, remarks,

> Indeed, even in my own life, when entering religious life prior to Vatican II, it was in truth a withdrawal from the world (even though we stepped into it to teach or nurse). The writings of Teresa of Avila and John of the Cross were kept in locked bookcases. To even desire to read them was thought to be dangerously close to spiritual pride and delusion. To meditate—yes! To practice virtue—of course! To work hard and with dedication—absolutely! But to aspire to mysticism—never![21]

Many of us have a false notion of mysticism. We think of those who have unusual experiences such as levitations, visions, and the stigmata, which remove them as credible guides for our rather ordinary lives. Or we think of those who suffered incredible hardships in Jesus' name. Why would we want to become one? Yet mystics are people just like you and me who, within the particular circumstances in their life, fall in love with God deeply, personally, and intimately. Such love then compels them to serve their neighbor, knowing that in loving their neighbor, even their enemy, they are, in fact, loving God.

Does such love cost? Of course, but what else makes life worthwhile?

One mystic whose spirituality deals with the paradoxes of life is the sixteenth-century Carmelite priest and saint, John of the Cross. I find that his teaching on the dark night of the soul provides insight and guidance for those of us searching for a substantive spirituality to guide us through the second half of life.[22]

John of the Cross

John of the Cross's life illustrates for us an important truth—human experience, in addition to Scripture and tradition, is a source of revelation. The image "Dark Night" welled up from the depth of his being as he languished in a dark closet. He had been kidnapped by members of his own Carmelite community who were opposed to the reform of the order he had undertaken with Teresa of Avila. He was locked up for nine months in this small closet, six by ten feet, with one small window high in the wall. He had little to eat. He endured the extremes of weather, either unbearably hot or cold. He suffered in darkness, alone.

In the midst of this severe deprivation and isolation, he sought relief by composing poems in his mind. Here a synthesis began to take shape—one way to union with God moves through experiences of loss and emptiness to intimacy and union. John's writings do not originate from idle speculation, but in response to real events. What guidance does he provide us as we search for meaning in the experiences of loss, limitation, and emptiness as well as the joys and satisfaction of midlife and beyond?

First, John is not writing for beginners in the spiritual life. He writes for those who have lived the morning of life and now find themselves in a new place in their spiritual lives. Indeed John writes for those who have experienced the best of what life has to offer—health, happy marriage, fulfilling job—and yet find themselves still wanting. One woman writes,

> I have been so blessed. I have a wonderful husband, loving children, a fulfilling job. But at the strangest times I feel this overwhelming ache...what's missing?[23]

He also writes for those of us who have experienced the disillusionment of our dreams—the limitations of marriage, disappointments from children, the shattered expectations of job fulfillment. John wants us to name these experiences and recognize them for what they are. No one, not anything, can ultimately fulfill the deepest longings of our hearts other than God. Each one of us eventually has to claim with Augustine, "*My* heart is restless until it rests in You, O my God."

Transformation of Desire

Many of us never quiet ourselves long enough to truly consider what we really want. We don't make time for quiet and reflection. Recently, a woman told me about her first directed retreat at a Jesuit spirituality center. The person guiding her retreat asked her to consider the question: What are your deepest desires? No one had ever asked her that before.

In his writings, John answers that question: God is our deepest desire. God creates us out of love, for the purpose of love, as the fulfillment of our love. The problem is that we don't realize who we are and for what we are made. Over time, due to our own weakness and sin, we misplace that love. We attach it to persons, behaviors, things as ends in themselves, expecting them to satisfy the deepest longings of our hearts. And they do, up to a point, for they "whisper to us of God" who is the origin of all our loves.[24] John describes the work of the Holy

Spirit as a transformation of our desire, moving us (if we choose to cooperate) from this self-centered, possessive, ego-centered love to a mature, free, self-giving love which orders all our loves toward and in our love for God.

The Dark Night of the Soul

John describes God as a lavish God who desires to give himself to us. God's purpose is to make the soul *grande*—great. To accomplish this goal, the Holy Spirit provokes, invites, and perseveres until we are wide enough and open enough to receive the gift of total union with God. Allowing God to stretch us, creating space for God to fill, entails a purification which John describes as a "dark night of the soul."

This dark night is experienced as two movements: the dark night of the *senses* and the dark night of the *spirit*. The dark night of the senses takes place in the realm of our sensate experiences—sight, smell, touch, hearing, taste. It happens to many of us and is a difficult experience. The dark night of the spirit takes place in the realm of intellect, memory, and love. This experience happens to fewer people and is much more difficult.

Dark Night of the Senses

We are concerned at the midlife stage of our lives with the meaning of the dark night of the senses. John wants us to recognize that we all begin family life, ministry, and work with great desires. We may spend many years experiencing the satisfaction of these desires. This is how life should be. Yet the time will come when we experience limits, the inability of our choices to satisfy us in the way they did before: A job no longer energizes us as it once did; a marriage once full of newness and mystery now seems stale, routine, or less stimulating; a ministry that once gave purpose to our lives now seems burdensome.

Since prayer is never separate from life, what was once full of consolation—liturgy, Eucharistic adoration, meditation—now feels empty. The God we experienced as the God of consolation now seems distant. What is happening?

John wants us to understand that these experiences of limit, void, and emptiness in our lives and in our relationship with God do not necessarily mean there is something wrong with our prayer or our commitments. Rather, they are signs that we are undergoing a time of purification and maturation in our marriage, ministry, or relationship with God. We are being challenged to make the passage from loving, serving, "being with" because of the pleasure and joy it gives us, to loving and serving regardless of cost.

In her book *Awakening to Prayer* Clare Wagner expresses the depth and anguish of this purification process in her own midlife crisis:

> In my own life, this passage involved a serious vocational crisis and a drastic shift in my image and understanding of God. This process includes staying with confusion, broken heartedness, a sense of hopelessness and uncertainty. That said, the movement is also toward freedom, depth and integrity. You are led where you would rather not go. However, you and God create a more authentic self.[25]

Our participation with God in creating a more authentic self is filled with challenges. Our culture does not encourage us to stay with situations that are difficult or confusing. Every advertisement promotes instant gratification. Consequently, we are tempted to look for external ways to replenish our interior wasteland: frenetic activity, addictions to shopping, alcohol, or prescription drugs; overinvolvement in the lives of our children, students, coworkers. But John challenges us to stay with the darkness, the emptiness, the confusion, and let it work out its purification and maturation in us. A forty-three-year-old woman named Marianne, living with the aftermath of a difficult divorce writes,

> I can absolutely attest to the fact that whatever issues are not recognized, confronted, accepted and resolved in the various stages of human development, will emphatically make themselves known and demand clarification at whatever cost to the individual. In my spiritual journey at this time of my life, I am in the clearing in the woods.

I look back at the forest I have just come out of, that dark, scary forest, filled with the "demons" and the "strange noises" from a myriad of painful experiences beginning with my early childhood, and I wonder how I ever found my way out of it. But of course, I know now, that the God I was desperately searching for and who seemed so distant and non-existent was leading the way.[26]

Marianne is challenged to face painful childhood experiences that impact her ability to trust others. To make matters worse, God seems remote. Yet she stays with the darkness and works through her demons. She gradually realizes that God was with her all the way along, strengthening her resolve, showing her the way out.

The tragedy for many of us is that we refuse to make this passage to greater self-knowledge. Life experiences bring us up against issues in ourselves that we don't want to face, so we continue to turn away from them. We refuse the call to deeper maturity within ourselves and our relationships. John tells us that even though it feels terrible, the darkness holds the promise of a new life, a new vision and experience of God, of self, and of others.

Marianne describes the promise of new life on the other side of the dark night:

So now I am in the clearing; I am catching my breath so to speak, resting in the quiet, listening. I am discovering the Jesus who led me through the woods and I am discovering my real self. I don't think Jesus could work through my "false" self—I couldn't work with myself! But I now know that God loves me and those times I cried out, "Help" and thought I was hopelessly lost in the woods were the times He took my hand and said, "This is the way out." My resting in this quiet, sunlit place is not so much a reward or consolation as it is a gathering of strength, of becoming rooted in my faith and in Jesus.[27]

Marianne describes what John of the Cross refers to as the active and passive experiences of the dark night. Both address what we identify today as "habits of the heart." Many of our habits are good—healthy diet, regular exercise, positive thought patterns, prayer, and reflection. Other habits are ultimately bad for us—perfectionism, negative patterns of thinking, unhealthy relationships, consumerism, frenetic activity, overwork, alcoholism. John describes them as *inordinate* attachments, for they reduce our freedom and impede our growth in a relationship with God and others.

The active experience of the dark night concerns what *we* do to rid ourselves of our unhealthy attachments. President George W. Bush described his battle with alcohol as a competition between two loves. His love of alcohol competed with his love for his wife and family. He eventually had to choose. I'm sure we all can name similar choices in our own lives. They involve a process of getting our house in order—an image most women can relate to—an uncluttering, a right ordering, a letting go of false gods that sap our energy for true self-giving love for God and others.

The passive experience of the dark night refers to what *God* does to heal our unhealthy patterns of thought and behavior. When Marianne thought she was hopelessly lost in the woods, God took her by the hand and showed her the way out. God brought her to more genuine self-knowledge, a stronger faith, and a new level of freedom to love herself and others—a clearing in the woods she could not find on her own. John speaks of this time as the inflow of God's love into our lives. Unfortunately, we don't feel God's presence at the time. Only in hindsight do we realize God was there all the time.

The scriptural passage which describes the dark night of the senses is the story of the rich man who put the question to Jesus, "Good Teacher, what must I do to inherit eternal life?" He obviously is a good Jew, for he has followed the law "from my earliest days." Jesus looked steadily at him, "loved him, and said, 'You lack one thing; go, sell what you own, and give the money to the poor, and you will have treasure in heaven; then come, follow me.' When he heard this he was shocked and went away grieving, for he had many possessions" (Mark 10:17, 21–22).

The problem here is not that the man had great wealth, but that the wealth *owned* him. It limited his freedom and impeded his ability to respond to Jesus' invitation to closer companionship. The same is true for us. To what degree does our wealth—all that we receive through our senses: material goods, relationships, career—diminish or expand our ability to become our true selves in God? Rather than diverting us from loving God and others, John's point is that all the goods of the earth are meant to be seen as gifts, as sacraments by which God comes to us and through which we return the gift of ourselves to God. Who knows? Maybe this man whom Jesus loved had second thoughts. Maybe he returned to Jesus and offered him his wealth to be put in the service of Jesus' mission. But John is clear. God loves and respects our freedom too much to intrude where not invited.

In her classic little book, *Gift from the Sea*, Anne Morrow Lindbergh describes this journey from death to new life from a woman's perspective. She notes that middle-aged experiences of discontent, restlessness, doubt, and longing are interpreted falsely as signs of decay. She acknowledges that many women prefer to deny what she views as paradoxical signs that presage both life and death. "Anything rather than stand still and learn from them. One tries to cure the signs of growth, to exorcise them, as if they were devils, when really they might be angels of annunciation." These angels announce the possibility of "a new stage in living…free at last for spiritual growth."[28]

"Free at last for spiritual growth" is the coming of the dawn after the dark night. The fruit of these years often reveal women at their best. There is an integration that was not present before. One woman writes, "When you emerge on the other side, the light seems brighter, the birdsong sweeter and the dappling in the water more beautiful. You see the world with new eyes because of the darkness behind you. You have arrived at a new place further on in your journey."[29] We emerge with a stronger, more authentic sense of self; a more compassionate and less judgmental attitude toward others; a deeper love and trust in God as the fulfillment of our deepest desires. We find ourselves more peaceful in our profession, religious community, single life, marriage. We are often motivated to share God's love and compassion for others in a real, practical service in the world.

The Autumn of Life

The decade of the forties began with a midlife transition or crisis that inaugurated a period of reassessment of our lives: Who have we become? What have we accomplished? What relationships are important? How much time do we have left to realize our dreams and deepen the meaning of our lives? Where has God been in the first half of our lives? How has God invited us to new growth and maturity through the opportunities and challenges of this morning of our lives?

As we come to the end of our forties, we need to bring the reassessment of our lives to a close and lay the groundwork for our middle years. Either we recommit ourselves in a deeper way to commitments already made, or we create a new life structure that promises deeper meaning and purpose. One woman recently commented to me, "The fifties have been good to me. They are good years for women." Would you agree? Let us move to the next chapter where we explore the final decade of the autumn years.

FOOD FOR THOUGHT

1. What was your experience of midlife, the halfway point of your life? Was it a difficult time or did you sail through it without much thought?

2. Did you have a midlife transition or crisis? If so, what changes did you make to prepare for a more meaningful future?

3. Does faith as paradoxical resonate with your response to God at this time in your life?

4. Does John of the Cross's dark night of the senses provide a helpful framework for understanding the challenges and graces of the spiritual journey at the midpoint of our lives? What did you find most meaningful?

REFLECTION

O guiding night!
O night more lovely than the dawn!
O night that has united
The lover with his beloved
Transforming the beloved in her lover.
This guided me
More surely than the light of noon
To where he waited for me—him I knew so well—
In a place where no one appeared. [30]

—John of the Cross

PRAYER

"Sometimes I wonder what I might say if I were to meet You in person, Lord. I might say, 'Thank You, Lord, for always being there for me. I know with certainty there were times when you carried me, when through your strength I got through the dark times in my life.'" [31]

CHAPTER THREE

* THE AUTUMN OF LIFE: INTENTIONAL FAITH *

> You come to a place in your life when what
> you've been is going to form what you will be.
> If you've wasted what you have in you, it is
> too late to do much about it. If you've invested
> yourself in life, you're pretty certain to get a
> return. If you are inwardly a serious person,
> in the middle years it will pay off. [1]
> —Lillian Hellman

It is now late autumn. The weather is no longer warm. The days have gotten shorter, the sky grayer. The brilliant shades of orange, yellow, and red have faded from the leaves. The grass is dormant and no longer needs to be cut. The squirrels gather their food for the winter; the birds fly south. The chill in the air reminds us that winter is right around the corner, and we begin to prepare for its challenges. Where are we in our journey toward human and spiritual integration as the season of autumn draws to a close? Women who invested themselves in resolving the issues of midlife prepare for their fifties by a recommitting to their present life, or to forming a new one in which to meet the joys, tasks, and graces of this new decade. For the inwardly serious woman, the payoff involves becoming more fully her authentic self.

Individuation—the process of growing into a genuine sense of self that gives a distinctive character to our lives—is a lifelong process. It is not to be equated with individualism—the self-centeredness and ego-centricity that is rampant in our society. On the contrary, individuation involves a balance of responsibility to and for others with responsibility to and for oneself.

When reflecting on the opportunities and struggles of middle life, most of us probably would not think to use the image of "polarities." Yet, in his conversations with women and men, Levinson heard them describe what psychiatrist Carl Jung referred to as the "reconciliation of opposites" in the psyche. Jung maintained that the psyche contains polarities of energy which we experience as opposites. Beginning with midlife and into middle adulthood, we are challenged to integrate these opposites as we move toward greater realization of the self.

Levinson identified four polarities that take center stage during middle adulthood: young/old; destruction/creation; masculine/feminine; attachment/separation. This chapter describes these polarities and explores key theological themes that interpret them within the context of our faith.

As I have noted many times throughout the book, God comes to us in the opportunities and struggles of each season of life. Hopefully a description of these polarities of energy as they find expression in lives of women in their fifties and early sixties will enable us to live our faith more *intentionally* as God guides us to greater wholeness and holiness.

Poet and spiritual writer Kathleen Norris makes the observation that many adults who would not dream of relying on the understanding of literature or science they acquired as children, in their adulthood are all too often content to leave their juvenile theological convictions largely unexamined. As a result, they are at a loss to explain why a child's view of their faith does not answer their adult questions about the meaning of life and death.[2] An underdeveloped theology leads to a distorted spirituality. We want to make sure that the theology that undergirds our spirituality can sustain us through the second half of life. The integration of the four polarities should lead to a more genuine experience of God.

The Young/Old Polarity

Levinson maintains that in their fullest meaning, the terms "young" and "old" are not tied to specific age levels. They are symbols that refer to basic psychological, biological, and social qualities in every season of life. We are both young and old at every age. "Young" represents birth, growth, possibility, openness, and potential. Conversely, "old" symbolizes fruition, stability, completion, and, ultimately, death.

Being young and old at the same time is inherent in the very nature of developmental transitions. We feel old in that phase of our lives that is ending and must be permitted to pass, yet young as we begin each new stage in life with its potential for growth. I remember my then–fourteen-year-old daughter telling me how old she felt when she graduated from grade school! And yet, how nervous and excited she felt at the thought of entering the new, unknown world of high school. Looking forward to the new season that is beginning becomes more daunting as we grow older. The task, then, is to reconcile the young/old polarity in a way that is appropriate to this particular season of the lifecycle.[3]

One woman captures the "young" side of the polarity when she states, "I find myself confident about life and its decisions. I take one day at a time. I feel very peaceful, very loving and very positive about my life, and the lives of my husband and my two children."[4] We feel this woman's enthusiasm and optimism for this time of her life. Another woman reflects the opposite pole as she considers the reality of aging and with it, facing her mortality,

> Turning thirty held no special onus for me; the same with forty. But fifty! Fifty seems to hold something fearsome, something lurking. It comes in large measure from seeing those "anchors" in the generation

WEAVING FAITH AND EXPERIENCE

ahead of me (parents and their contemporaries) aging and then dying; those whom we relied upon to care for the world, for us, for me. This leaves me and my contemporaries edging closer to the mysterious precipice of death. In a word, I now come closer to facing my own mortality.[5]

The young/old polarity, then, finds expression in our personal attitude toward growing older and the quality of life we choose to live at this time. Our efforts to integrate this polarity in a healthy way are further influenced by how the young/old dynamic is viewed in society.

Many women maintain that society's stereotype of the middle-aged woman does not help the integration process. Psychologist Juanita Williams describes how middle-aged women appear in fairy tales as wicked stepmothers or witches, almost never as normal, mature women:

> Ugly to the point of deformity, their personalities are distorted by jealousy and hatred, they have a penchant for cruelty, especially toward young girls, as in "Cinderella" and "Sleeping Beauty." If fairy tales, like myths, are made in the deep layers of the mind, out of the oldest fears and ruminative concerns of humans, then we see in them the reflections of fear and dread toward aging and toward the woman who is no longer young.[6]

But wait, you may protest, the baby-boomer generation has changed all that! Women today take better care of themselves, they look younger longer, they stay active and involved. Middle-aged women are perceived more positively by younger generations. After all, the fifties are the new forties! While this is true, do not middle-aged women still receive a mixed message from a society obsessed with youth?

The 2007 fairy tale, the popular Disney movie *Enchanted,* captured in a contemporary mode the feelings of fear and dread toward the woman who is no longer young. Giselle is a princess ejected from her magic kingdom by the curse of her evil, ugly, middle-aged, potential mother-in-law, Queen Narissa. Giselle has been conceived thematically and visually after the classic Disney heroines Snow White and Cinderella. Each waits to be rescued by her prince. In order to maintain control over her son, Queen Narissa comes to earth (Times Square, no less) and, in the guise of an ugly witch, persuades Giselle to eat an apple that will unite her to her one true love. Unfortunately, the apple is poisoned, and Giselle falls into a deep sleep. She is awakened by "love's true kiss." There is good news for young women in the ending of this fairy tale. Instead of the hero rescuing the heroine, the heroine saves her hero!

Yet, the stereotype of the wicked mother-in-law or stepmother who continues to be portrayed as an evil, ugly middle-aged woman, is reinforced for a new generation of young women. If fairy tales are made in the deepest layers of our cultural psyches, we still have a ways to go in portraying middle-aged women as vitally alive, happy in themselves, mentors to younger women, fulfilled by developing those qualities that get better with age—intellectual competence, wisdom, and compassion.

The young/old polarity also finds expression in what Levinson describes as a major issue in middle-age—our legacy. How do we want to be remembered? What do we want to pass on to future generations?

For a majority of women, the value of marriage and family life constitutes their most prized legacy. Yet, today, women have other options, too.

One is philanthropy. Today more women are independently wealthy or partner with their husbands to distribute funds to organizations that benefit poor women and children, the environment, or education. Other women consider their work as their major legacy—art, science, writing, research—work that constitutes a treasure that can live forever in their name. Still other women are employed in influential professions as doctors, judges, school counselors, teachers, nurses, or administrators of hospitals and nursing homes—occupations that leave a legacy of healing, teaching, and comforting that create better lives for future generations. The wish to create a legacy enriches our lives in middle adulthood—often our most productive years. What do you want to be remembered for? What will be your legacy?

A Theology of Faith

Jesus provides us with a description of the quality of faith that can guide our integration of the young/old polarity. In Mark's Gospel we read that people bring little children to be touched by Jesus. The disciples turn them away. But when Jesus saw this, he was indignant and said to them, "Let the little children come to me; do not stop them; for it is to such as these that the kingdom of God belongs. Truly I tell you, whoever does not receive the kingdom of God as a little child will never enter it" (Mark 10:14–15). In this passage, Jesus is inviting us to live out of a child*like*, not a child*ish*, faith. No matter where we are in the integration of the young/old polarity, the unconditional love and trust that we see in children model the qualities of a lively faith. One woman shared with me that she often hears Jesus say that he believes in her more than she believes in him. Could Jesus say the same to us as well? Life in a secular society has a way of testing this childlike faith. Rather than succumbing to the cynicism and skepticism that occur when God seems distant or uninvolved, Jesus asks us to trust, to have childlike faith in him. It is to such individuals that the kingdom of God belongs.

Saint Paul also helps us put the young/old polarity in perspective. "Even though our outer nature is wasting away, our inner nature is being renewed day by day" (2 Corinthians 4:16). In the course of our development, we peak physically around age twenty-five. Then begins the slow, or for some, quick, deterioration of our bodies. A critical task of middle and late adulthood is to recognize that as the body slowly declines, our spirit should be growing, so that when we die, we are all spirit and little body. Those who do not attend to this process of developing a spiritual life are often the ones who have the hardest time facing death.

A friend of mine, Elaine, was diagnosed with Lou Gehrig's disease at the age of fifty-five. She was the life of the party: vivacious, full of energy, with a great sense of humor. Her speech gave out first, followed by the gradual deterioration of her neurosystem, and then her entire body. She was a woman of faith who responded to this devastating disease with courage and grace. When her brother-in-law reflected on her life in his eulogy, he said, "Whenever I went to visit Elaine, it was evident that her body was being destroyed by this disease, but when you looked into her eyes, you could see her spiritual strength increase day by day." The eyes, it is said, are the windows of the soul. He recognized that through her illness, Elaine responded with a deep, intentional faith. In the process she was sanctified.

Another expression of the young/old polarity is the opportunity to leave a legacy of our faith. There are numerous women throughout the history of the church who have left us a legacy about what it means to follow Christ. We are invited to do the same.

Robert Ellsberg's *Blessed Among All Women* is a rich compendium of women "who struggled hard to assert their full humanity and to follow God where God was calling them, even when they challenged the prevailing options of the time."[7] Ellsberg groups the legacies of these women according to the beatitudes—Jesus' summary of the spirit of discipleship. Some left a legacy of dying for their faith with grace and courage; others left a legacy of active apostolic work among the poor and forgotten; some engaged in missionary endeavors as they traveled across the world to proclaim the gospel, or created or led religious communities that educated, healed, and ministered to people. Some women created new approaches to theology or spirituality; still others wrote about their experiences of God to guide others. Many women left a legacy of opposing slavery, war, and social injustice. Ellsberg reminds us that the story of each woman is really a story about God. What greater legacy could we have? As women of faith, creating such a legacy is within the reach of all of us.

The Destruction/Creation Polarity

As we review our lives and consider how to give them greater meaning, we are invited to come to terms in a new way with destruction and creation as fundamental aspects of our lives. Integrating this polarity increases in intensity as we enter the autumn of our lives.

In assessing our lives, we seek to better understand the grievances we have against others for the real or imagined damage they have done to us. Hurts from childhood, suppressed in adolescence and early adulthood, now return and demand our attention. The anger or disappointment we feel toward parents, husband, siblings, children, employers, or colleagues who have hurt us is very real and, at times, frightening. We may be surprised by the rage we feel and struggle with what to do with it. One woman writes,

> The challenge of this time in my life is accepting my age, where I am in life and dealing with the overwhelming anger I sometimes feel toward certain people and occurrences in my life. I know I must learn how to forgive myself and others, but it is very hard.[8]

As this woman indicates, not only must we come to terms with the destructive effects others have had on our lives, but we also need to acknowledge the destructive effects we have had on others and on ourselves. We can be filled with self-blame and self-hatred. How have we hurt those closest to us? How have we hurt people with whom we work? And how have we been destructive toward ourselves?

These questions bring to mind what Carl Jung calls the shadow—the neglected, negative side of our personality. The shadow provides a framework for discussing the possible sources of destruction within the psyche. Jung described individuation as the integration of the conscious and unconscious dimensions of the psyche in the discovery of the true self. He maintained that we can't develop all aspects of our personality at the same time. Normally, we develop those parts of ourselves that are most dominant and are affirmed by our family, friends, and society.

However, as we have seen, "voices from the other rooms" of our psyche—those underdeveloped or feared parts of ourselves—demand to be heard in midlife. Some of those voices represent aspects of our personality that we are ashamed of, or recognize as unacceptable to our conscious personality, family, and society. Jung wrote, "Unfortunately there can be no doubt that [man] is, on the whole less good than he imagines himself or wants to be. Everyone carries a shadow, and the less it is embodied in the individual's conscious life, the *blacker* and denser it is."[9] If the contents of the shadow are not consciously met and allowed room in the personality, the pent-up energy becomes destructive and controls the personality in an unconscious manner. As Sigmund Freud, the founder of the science of psychology, once observed, "What you don't own, owns you."

When we don't integrate the shadow, we tend to project it onto someone else, often someone of the same sex. For example, if we tend to be emotional in our response to situations, we may ridicule a woman who is cool under pressure. If we are timid around other people, we may put down a woman who socializes easily with other people. When we find ourselves overreacting to something in another woman, our shadow has been hooked. By falsely assigning a negative quality in ourselves to someone else, we escape the need to deal with it in ourselves. Jungian psychiatrist Jolande Jacobi describes this experience:

> It is in ourselves that we most frequently and readily perceive shadow qualities, provided we are willing to acknowledge them as belonging to ourselves; for example, when an outburst of rage comes over us, when suddenly we begin to curse or behave crudely, when quite against our will we act antisocially, when we are stingy, petty, or choleric, cowardly, frivolous, or hypocritical, so displaying qualities which under ordinary circumstances we carefully hide or repress....When the emergence of such traits of character can no longer be overlooked, we ask ourselves in amazement: How was it possible? Is it really true that things like this are me?[10]

Such a moment of truth can have a positive effect on the rest of our journey. Once we withdraw the projection by owning it in ourselves, we reduce its power over us, and can redirect that energy into areas of growth and development.

The shadow does not represent only negative projections. We can also project positive qualities of the self on to others. It is far easier to admire a quality like self-discipline in another than to do the work required to develop it in ourselves. Yet, to demand that another live out qualities that we don't acknowledge in ourselves is to sabotage our own movement toward wholeness and health.

The shadow, then, represents both a destructive and a creative polarity within the psyche. We don't have to be familiar with Jung's concept of the shadow in order to deal with unowned aspects of ourselves, but we are accountable to grow in self-knowledge, one of the fundamental principles of human and spiritual growth. The more we understand how the psyche works, the more capable we are of choosing good and avoiding destructive patterns of behavior. It is well worth reflecting on how the shadow finds expression in our lives and how we are challenged by certain women who represent what we don't like, or don't want to take responsibility for, in our own lives.

A concrete example of the destruction/creation polarity for women is menopause. The average age of menopause for American women is fifty. Some women live through menopause with no symptoms. Others have mild to serious symptoms that include hot flashes, night sweats, sleep difficulties, and irritability.

There are a variety of responses to this female rite of passage. One forty-six-year-old woman represents the perspective of women who, in an attempt to put off that fateful day, announces her pregnancy with the remark, "Just nipped through the door before the shop shut."[11] Another speaks for many when she admits that even though she would not want to have another child, she grieves the loss of this privileged opportunity to create life. Another woman expresses heartfelt relief, acknowledging that once she and her husband had the number of children they wanted, she could not enjoy sexual intercourse due to the anxiety over the thought of another pregnancy.

Recent research confirms that middle-aged women generally have a positive attitude toward menopause. For most women it signals the end of one kind of birthing, only to usher in the opportunity to create in a variety of new ways. One woman writes, "Menopause signaled a new beginning for me. With my childbearing years behind me, I have renewed energy to pursue lots of activities that I had placed on hold."[12]

In middle adulthood, then, we come to know that powerful forces of destruction and creation coexist within us. We need to come to terms with their expression in our lives. Most importantly, where necessary, we need to forgive ourselves and others so we can move on with a sense of purpose and creative involvement in the relationships and activities that provide meaning and purpose for our lives.

A Theology of Sin and Grace

A theology of sin and grace helps us interpret the destruction/creation polarity within the context of faith. The Greek word for *sin* is *hamartia* —to miss the mark. At times we are tempted to look at the evil in ourselves and in the world and say, "Well, we're only human," but that is a cop-out. To miss the mark reminds us that there is a way of being human that we have failed to measure up to. We are made in the image and likeness of God and God expects us to act accordingly. When we act selfishly, we distort our original goodness. It is important for us to recognize that the negative aspects of the shadow side of our personality, which we explored earlier, are not synonymous with sin. They can become sin, however, when they lead us to do unloving things.

Our ability to forgive ourselves and others depends, in part, on our image of God. If our image is a negative one—God as punisher, policeman, judge, stern father, old white man in the sky—it can block our ability to grow in our relationship with God. One image of God that has been destructive in the lives of many women is God as a malevolent being who sends us suffering or is the cause of the death of our loved ones. Recently five teenagers were killed when their car collided with a passenger train. Guardrails were down; lights were flashing. The young man who was driving the car was late for work. He pulled out from behind two cars and tried to beat the train. All five passengers in the car were killed instantly. Newspaper comments from the family and friends included: "God must have had a plan in taking their lives"; "Why would God do this to five teenagers who had such promising lives ahead of them?" The operative image of God here is the puppeteer who pulls the strings directing the flow of our lives.

This image of God is contrary to the God revealed in Jesus. We blame God for many things in life that are contrary to God's will. It is well to remember that the God revealed in Jesus is above all a God who respects our freedom; a God of love who intends only our well-being, wholeness, and health. God's promise is to be with us in situations of sin, brokenness, suffering, and death to help us choose life, however difficult that might be. The theological language for God's presence in our lives is grace.

I want to call attention to three distinct but related meanings of a theology of grace. First, grace means giving thanks, being filled with gratitude. Second, grace refers to a gift freely given and received. Third, grace refers to the giver of the gift: God. In the Middle Ages, Christianity emphasized the second meaning over the third—the created gift of God seemed more tangible than God as the giver of the gift. I suspect that the operative theology of grace for many of us is still found in the second meaning. We go to liturgy and receive the sacraments to "get grace"; that is, receive the gift of the Giver.

The Catholic theologian most responsible for an important shift in our understanding of grace is Karl Rahner. He emphasized the third meaning of grace: Grace is the self-giving communication of God's very being to our being through the gift of the Holy Spirit. The Holy Spirit, the very Spirit that was in Jesus, joins our spirit. The Holy Spirit prods and encourages us to integrate the polarities that take center stage at this time of our lives so that we become more fully our true selves in God. This integration takes place in what Rahner calls the mysticism of everyday life. A radio interviewer told Rahner that he had never had an experience of God. Rahner responded emphatically, "I don't believe you; I just don't accept that. You have had, perhaps, no experience of God under this precise code-word, *God,* but you have had or have now an experience of God—and I am convinced that this is true of every person."[13]

In his brief essay "Experiencing the Spirit," Rahner describes two distinct types of God experience: one positive and the other negative. Positive experiences are moments when we experience a deep-felt joy in just being alive; when we drink deeply of surpassing natural beauty; the sheer joy at our cocreativity with God in the birth of a child; an experience of unconditional love when we don't feel worthy of such love; fidelity and self-sacrifice for family, shown in getting up each morning to attend to their needs. These are experiences of grace.[14]

Negative experiences occur when things fall apart and people fail us; when life is full of fear, suffering, difficulty, pain, and loss. Grace transforms these moments, allowing us to forgive after weeks of hardness of heart; to remain silent rather than strike back; to offer a kind word to someone who has deeply offended us; to continue to care for a loved one inflicted with a debilitating disease. One of the most moving experiences of grace in one of the most horrific human conditions possible is found in the diary of Etty Hillesum, who was killed in Auschwitz at the age of twenty-nine:

> It is possible to suffer with dignity and without. I mean, most of us in the West don't understand the art of suffering and experience a thousand fears instead. We cease to be alive, being full of fear, bitterness, hatred and despair. God knows, it is only too easy to understand why. But...I am in Poland every day, on the battlefields, if that's what one can call them. I often see visions of poisonous green smoke; I am with the hungry, with the ill-treated and the dying, every day, but I am also with the jasmine and with that piece of sky beyond my window; there is room for everything in a single life.... I sometimes bow

my head under the great burden that weighs down on me, but even
as I bow my head I also feel the need, almost mechanically, to fold
my hands. And so I can sit for hours and know everything and bear
everything and grow stronger in the bearing of it, and at the same
time feel sure that life is beautiful and worth living and meaningful.
Despite everything.[15]

Surrounded by suffering, Hillesum affirmed that life is still beautiful and
worth living. Rahner insists that this ability cannot be accounted for by
natural goodness. Rather, it discloses within itself the presence of a loving God from whom this response originates. All of us have such experiences of God, but too often we miss the meaning. We may recognize
God's presence in hindsight when we become aware of a presence—a
felt sense that Someone beyond ourselves was at work in our lives.

All the challenges we have examined in our discussion of the four
polarities of our lives—the challenge of aging in a culture obsessed with
youth; the opportunity to create a legacy; the difficulty of gaining the
self-knowledge that comes from owning our shadow; the choice of how
we deal with menopause, empty nests, and retirement—all these are
catalysts for spiritual growth, because God is right in the midst of
them, encouraging us to choose generativity over stagnation; growth,
maturity and self-knowledge over decline, immaturity, and defeat. Our
theology of sin and grace is at the heart of how we deal with the polarities of life in our journey to wholeness.

Masculine/Feminine Polarity

The masculine/feminine is the third polarity in Levinson's study. First,
a clarification of terms: "male" and "female" refer to biological genders.
A male is a boy in pre-adulthood; a man in adulthood. A female is a girl
and then a woman. The terms "masculine" and "feminine" refer to the
meaning we give to gender. Levinson points out that the images of the
masculine and feminine are contained in all religions, political ideolo-
gies, family patterns, and social institutions. In the course of our lives all

of us receive powerful messages regarding the qualities and roles associated with both genders from our family, friends, religions, educational, political, cultural institutions, and especially today, the media.

In patriarchal societies, there has been a rigid splitting along gender lines: Men are masculine, women are feminine, and no one can be both. This split operates on many levels: the domestic sphere vs. the public sphere; "women's work" vs. "men's work"; feminine vs. masculine in the individual psyche. During the last several hundred years we have witnessed a slow reduction in these ancient gender distinctions. There is greater recognition that women are not categorically different from men, that they have similar desires as men and can develop many of the same skills. Of course, gender assignments vary significantly from country to country. A continuing area of debate among scientists is the nature vs. nurture issue; that is, the degree of influence to be assigned to basic biological differences between women and men on the one hand, and various social-psychological meanings of gender on the other. The meaning a society gives to masculinity and femininity has a powerful influence on women's and men's self-perception, development, and life direction.

What does it mean to be "masculine" and "feminine"? What personal qualities do we associate with each? Most of the men in Levinson's study described what we would call a traditional splitting of the masculine and feminine along gender lines. They viewed men as strong, independent, powerful, logical, athletic, ambitious, and competitive. They viewed women as weak, unassertive, emotional, intuitive, relational, passive, empathetic, and nurturing. During their young years, most of the men clung to the rigid separation of qualities. As they matured and became more critical of cultural stereotypes, they were more open to acknowledging and developing what culture identified as feminine qualities.[16]

In his book *The Evolving Self,* Dr. Robert Kegan describes a more promising perspective on masculinity/femininity for interpreting contemporary experience.[17] Kegan maintains that two tendencies are built

into the human psyche. One is the drive toward relationality. It refers
to our yearning to be included, to be part of, close to, intimate with, to
be held, and accompanied. The other is the drive toward autonomy. It
refers to our yearning to be independent, self-reliant, distinctive, and
separate. Though these seem to be in conflict, it is their relationship, the
lifelong tension between the two that facilitates in many ways our
growth toward wholeness and integration.

Rather than view men as more independent and women as more
relational, Kegan suggests that each stage in life involves an evolution-
ary truce between the two. The life histories he has studied and the
individuals he has worked with reveal a continual moving back and
forth between resolving the tension in favor of autonomy at one stage
and relationality the next. Human maturity involves the continual rene-
gotiation of differentiation and integration, autonomy and inclusion.
Immaturity occurs when an individual becomes fixated or stuck in one
orientation to the exclusion of the other.

The value of Kegan's model of human development is the recognition of the equal dignity of both yearnings in women and men. He
emphasizes that there should be no question of one emphasis being
"better" than the other. He faults Western society for presenting male
development as the norm for human development, thereby favoring the
side of the polarity that men have felt more comfortable with: independence, self-assertion, aggrandizement, and personal achievement.
He maintains that this imbalance has been destructive to individuals
and to society as a whole. Furthermore, Kegan claims that there is little hope for well-being beyond midlife unless the traits stereotypically
reserved for one sex are assimilated by both.

Kegan's theory suggests that the qualities we have identified as
masculine and feminine are not innately more characteristic of one sex
or another, but rather are human qualities necessary for wholeness in
both sexes. In other words, when a woman is being assertive, she is not
developing her masculine side, but is activating the quality of assertive-

ness as a woman. Likewise, when a man is being nurturing, he is not exercising his feminine side, but is activating the quality of nurturing as a man.

Negotiating this integration is easier said than done. Psychologist Gail Sheehy, in a provocative article, "Hillaryland at War," in the August 2008 edition of *Vanity Fair*, maintains that when you try to make a man out of a woman you are bound to fail.[18] Sheehy asserts that during Hillary Clinton's presidential campaign, she was surrounded by men on her team who did not believe a woman could be elected president of the United States. Consequently, they portrayed her as a man. When other members of her team argued that Hillary's warmer, kinder, compassionate side needed to be displayed as well as her assertive, combative side, they would have none of it. Sheehy notes that in her concession speech, when it was too late, Hillary finally spoke as who she really is—"a woman full of humanity. Yes, ruthless, nakedly aggressive, hawkish, and often tone deaf—qualities common among those who dare to compete at this level. But she was also staggeringly smart, empathetic, unsparing in her energy and commitment, and gallant in her optimism."[19]

From Sheehy's perspective, the real disappointment was not discovering whether a woman, running as a woman, could be elected President of the United States.

Whether or not we agree with Sheehy's analysis, there is an important lesson here for women. Our contribution to the humanization of family, society, church, and world will not come from trying to act like a man. On the contrary, we need to work toward an integration of those qualities identified in the masculine/feminine polarity—the yearning for autonomy and a yearning for relationship—into our own unique expression of womanhood. The challenge facing women and men today is finding a way of being human in our maleness and femaleness that encourages mature mutuality in our personal relationships, family life, and societal and world interactions.

It may be instructive to ask ourselves: How does the drive toward autonomy and the drive toward relationality find expression in our lives? What is the favorable ratio between them? Are we comfortable with it or do we need to work on a better integration of the two?

A Theology of Christian Personhood

What bearing does the meaning we bring to male and female, masculine and feminine, have on how we see ourselves as women made in the image and likeness of God? How does the meaning we bring to both influence how we see ourselves as women, and how we relate to others and to God?

Our Catholic tradition offers three sets of answers to these questions. Thankfully the first, referred to as a dualistic approach, no longer undergirds church teaching. Dualism refers to the splitting apart of that which essentially belongs together. In this perspective, spirit and body were set against each other in men and women. Men's supposedly higher nature was equated with spirit and mind; women's lower nature, due to menstruation, childbearing, and menopause, with materiality and body. Since God is spirit, men were deemed superior and women inferior. Thus men by nature were nearer to the divine and capable of representing the divine in ways that women were not. For women to grow in relationship with God, they had to leave life in the body behind, and ascend into the life of the mind or spirit.

The second set of answers as to how we see ourselves as women and our relationship with others and with God is found in what is called a "complementary" approach to Christian personhood. Its contemporary expression is found in the teaching of John Paul II. Beginning with the first chapter of Genesis, John Paul notes that, unlike other creatures, the human person is defined on the basis of a relationship with God. This truth establishes the dignity and equality of all human beings. The pope states, "Both man and woman are human beings to an equal degree, both are created in God's image." Here women and men share a common humanity which is the basis for the fundamental equality between them. Central to this thought, John Paul emphasizes that this one nature is expressed in two different ways, male and female. In other words, women and men are equal insofar as they are human beings and complementary insofar as they are women and men.[20]

This complementarity expresses itself in specific qualities that are purportedly inherent in the nature of maleness and femaleness. For example, John Paul wrote that the unique essence of a woman lies in the notion that she is made for the "order of love." He stated, "Woman can only find herself by giving love to others.... It is she who receives love in order to love in return." In women's relationship with others and with God, John Paul emphasizes that the feminine genius is to be bearers of self-giving love, compassion, and peace. [21]

In relation to Robert Kegan's theory of human development, one could speculate that John Paul believed that the drive toward autonomy is constitutive of man's very being. Similarly, the drive toward relationality is inherent in the nature of femaleness. We are equal but different.

The third set of answers is found in what is called an "egalitarian partnership" approach. This position is espoused by theologians such as Sister Elizabeth Johnson and Dr. Anne Carr. This perspective recognizes that both men and women possess characteristics identified as masculine and feminine woven in a unique expression in each person. It views women, made in the image and likeness of God, as equal to men in their capability to symbolize God. While this approach also takes its cue from the first chapter of the book of Genesis, its point of emphasis is different from Pope John Paul II's.

While affirming the equality of women and men, its proponents point out that there is no assignment of masculine or feminine qualities here, but simply the fullness of being human persons in God's image in one's distinctive sexuality whether male or female. Consequently, Sister Elizabeth Johnson emphasizes that, "Diversity of personal characteristics and gifts are not predetermined by sex but ranges across a wide spectrum for women and men of all races and cultures. In fact, the full range of differences among women themselves can be just as great if not greater than differences between some women and men."[22] Johnson asserts that to suggest that certain qualities are a truer expression of woman's nature than of man's leads to the response of a male student in one of her courses: "Saying that women are more fitted to love means that they are better able to follow Jesus' teaching to love God and neighbor. Where does that leave me? Second-best?"[23] Johnson resists the move to understand women's and men's abilities as innate differences, for she believes that such a stance inevitably compromises the human and spiritual potential of both. From a theological perspective, Johnson's position would be closest to Dr. Robert Kegan's psychological model.

I began by asking how the meaning we bring to male and female, masculine and feminine, influences how we see ourselves as women and how we relate to others and to God. Each model we have described answers that question in a particular way. The dualistic approach conveys a negative attitude toward the body and materiality. Since women are identified with both, it suggests that women have to leave behind life in the body in order to enter into the realm of the spirit.

The complementary approach suggests that by being true to our specific nature as women, which is distinguished by a particular set of qualities, we realize our true selves in our relationship with others and with God. The egalitarian partnership approach contends that both men and women possess characteristics identified as masculine and feminine. The integration of those qualities as they find expression in each woman and man will lead to the realization of the true self in relationship with others and with God.

Whether we are aware of it or not, each one of us has internalized one of these perspectives on human personhood which influences how we see ourselves, and how we relate to others and to God. Whatever approach we espouse, we must do so intentionally out of a theology of

Christian personhood that commits us to working in partnership with a variety of women and men for the common good of the church and humanity.

Attachment/Separation Polarity

The final polarity to be addressed in middle life is the attachment/separation polarity. To be attached is to be engaged, rooted, involved, seeking, plugged in. In many ways attachment is what makes life worthwhile. We are attached to family, friends, work, particular causes, institutions, etc. These attachments bring us great joy and happiness; they also can cause deep pain and disappointment. At the opposite pole is separateness, which Levinson emphasizes is not the same as isolation or aloneness. A person is separate when she is primarily involved in her inner world—a world of imagination, fantasy, play, meditation, and prayer. For example, the professional novelist or composer at work is separate in that she is involved in her inner world, trying to create a product that is pleasing to her and expresses her thoughts and talents. Yet, she is also attached in that she hopes her work will be pleasing to a particular audience and will provide income and reputation.[24]

Persons of all ages and stages of development must deal with the attachment/separation polarity. If we are too separate, we may become isolated and lose touch with reality. If we become too attached to people, places, and things, we endanger our capacity for self-renewal, growth, and creative effort. While a balance between the two is important for each stage of life, one side of the polarity may necessarily be given more prominence in one stage than another. Developmental psychology emphasizes the importance of attachment throughout life, especially in the early, formative years. We now know that children who are not touched, cuddled, and caressed in the first three years of their lives may forever be unable to form deep attachments. Psychologist Erik Erikson reminds us that the need to experience a confirming face, not only at the beginning of life, but throughout all of life is "an ontogenetic requirement; that is, it is built into the very structure of who we are as human beings."[25] This undoubtedly provides one explanation as to why the scriptures are filled with longing to "see the face of God." One example,

> "Come," my heart says, "seek his face!"
> Your face, LORD, do I seek.
> Do not hide your face from me.
> (Psalm 27:8–9)

Our longing to see the face of God is answered in Jesus who has been described by many theologians down through the ages as "the face of God turned toward humanity."

Erikson also weighs in on developmental theory. Through the framework of generativity vs. stagnation, he describes the challenges of attachment and separation in the lives of middle-aged adults. Once again we see that growth comes from the creative tension of a dissonance within the self in relation to society. The task of generativity is to assume responsibility for others in a continuing way as only an adult can do. In other words, we are attached to our family, our community and our world in such a way that someone else's well-being becomes our chief concern. Erikson includes many forms of generativity as he describes women and men who have special gifts—such as celibate and single people who do not apply the drive of generativity to offspring, but to other forms of altruistic concerns and creativity that absorb their energy and responsibility.

The opposite end of the polarity is stagnation and self-absorption. When generativity fails, there is a compulsive preoccupation with self; an inability to get out of oneself; an inability to become attached, to care. Unfortunately there are many adults today who, rather than invest themselves in creating a better world for the next generation, become stuck in a narcissistic, self-serving way of life.[26]

What are some of the specific experiences of middle life that challenge as well as provide opportunities for the integration of this polarity? For married couples, the "empty nest" occurs when the last child leaves home. Once again there are a variety of responses to this experience. For many parents who invested a lifetime of self-giving love in raising their children, and have thoroughly enjoyed their children's companionship and activities, this experience of letting go and allowing children to get on with their own lives is very difficult. One woman writes, "I am dealing with a 'new' empty nest and feeling a great void in my personal and religious life. I'm lonely for our children, especially knowing that they will never live nearby. My husband and I don't have many couple friends. I'm at a loss."[27]

Some parents have a difficult time giving their children not only the physical, but the psychological space to live their own lives. But others, while they love their children, are now ready to get on with another chapter in their lives. Some couples discover that in the process of raising a family, they have grown apart. Their pattern of communication focuses on practical matters of household maintenance, while emotional needs go unmet. Long suppressed disappointment and resentment over the state of their marriage need to be addressed, but often neither party knows how to begin the conversation. In addition to these challenges, a faltering economy may mean that many empty nesters face the reality of a young adult returning home—a stressful situation that unexpectedly challenges the attachment/separation dynamic for all parties.

Another experience of the attachment/separation polarity is the need for multi-generational care experienced by what has become known as the "sandwich generation." These individuals are pulled in many directions, dividing their time between taking care of the needs of teenagers and young adults and the growing needs of aging parents. It can be an exhausting, stressful, and guilt-ridden time. There is just not enough time to meet the needs of everyone, not to mention the guilt that accompanies a decision to place a parent in a nursing home. The separation dimension of the polarity suffers when we do not take time to refuel mind, body, and spirit.

The issue of retirement also reconfigures the attachment/separation polarity in the lives of an individual or couple. For the person who chooses to retire, life is full of promise. Once unattached from the world of business, she is now free to pursue activities that renew the spirit—leisure, travel, hobbies, the enjoyment of being rather than doing. For the person who is forced to retire early, life can be full of anxiety and resentment that he is no longer considered a valuable asset to a business or an organization. An unwanted retirement tests a marriage as husband or wife returns home with little to do. One woman told me she considered divorce only when her husband retired. "He follows me around the house, telling me how to do chores that I've been handling very well for years!" The issue of retirement, then, can be a blessing or a curse in the attachment/separation polarity.

Thus, in the autumn of our lives, we strive to balance the attachment/separation polarity in many areas. We experience ourselves as deeply engaged and productive. We believe we have a set of skills, talents, insight, and wisdom that will enrich the lives of others. We resist the drive to get caught up in the contemporary addiction to busyness; to find our worth only in what we do. Anne Morrow Lindbergh reminds us,

> Certain springs are tapped only when we are alone. The artist knows she must be alone to create; the writer, to work out her thoughts; the musician, to compose; the saint to pray. Women need solitude in order to find again the true essence of themselves: that firm strand which will be the indispensable center of a whole web of human relationships.[28]

A healthy balance between solitude and engagement is found in a theology of communion.

A Theology of Communion

For Christian women and men, the indispensable center of the web of our relationships is our relationship with God. The attachment/separation polarity, from the perspective of our Christian faith, needs to be rooted in a theology of communion which recognizes our need for quiet time before God as well as a community of memory that reminds us who we are as Jesus' disciples in the world.

Some women justify their interest in spirituality and disengagement from a community of faith with the statement, "I am a spiritual person, but I'm not religious. I don't need the church." In severing connection with a community of memory, we lose a sense of identity and our link with Christians of every age. We risk the possibility of drifting into an unfocused, vague way of life that provides little nourishment and meaning.

Think about how our extended families influenced our identity. We may be Polish, Hispanic, Irish, African American, Asian, or German. These associations make up our heritage, histories, and traditions that provide us with an identity and a sense of belonging. When our family of origin doesn't provide it, we often go in search of it.

It is unfortunate when we take our communities of memory for granted. This awareness came home to me when my husband and I went to Russia to adopt our beautiful daughter, Victoria. The administrator of the orphanage told us what happens to the children who are not chosen for adoption. At the age of sixteen they are given a job and housing by the government. If for any reason they lose their job, they are on their own. They do not know their families of origin. They have no one to turn to for safety and protection. Many young men end up in prison for stealing or drug trafficking; many young women end up in prostitution. Few of us can imagine what living without any kind of community of memory would be like.

Christianity is one such community of memory. When Jesus asks us to "do this in memory of me," what are we being asked to do? We are being asked to live our lives after the pattern of Jesus' life. We are to wash one another's feet; we are to serve each other in self-giving love. Without this ongoing community of disciples, Jesus' mandate to preach and heal in his name will not be carried out.

In his book on Ignatian humanism, Ron Modras describes a life-sized crucifix he saw in a church in Germany. Large crosses are quite ordinary, except that the body of Jesus on this cross had no arms—a casualty of war. The parishioners decided to leave the crucifix in that truncated state as a reminder to onlookers that *they* are to become Christ's arms.[29]

Teresa of Avila expresses this same truth in a passage that provides motivation for many of us in our effort to be intentional Christians:

> Christ has no body now but yours no hands but yours, no feet but yours. Yours are the eyes through which Christ's compassion must look out on the world. Yours are the feet with which Christ is to go on about doing good. Yours are the hands with which He is to bless us now.[30]

We are Christ's eyes, his feet, his hands. Without us—a community of memory—a community of disciples—his memory dies, and with it a way of life that is meant to humanize a world so desperate for meaning, direction, and purpose.

In order to be a community of memory in Jesus' name, we need space for quiet reflection and renewal of spirit. The polarity of separation is not the same as isolation or aloneness. It refers to our need to be separate for the purpose of creativity and rejuvenation of body, mind, and spirit.

In the New Testament, we see Jesus concerned about this need for rest and renewal for his disciples. Mark tells us that one day the apostles gathered together with Jesus to report all that they had done and taught. Jesus said to them, "Come away by yourselves to a deserted place and rest a while." We know that Jesus periodically sought out quiet places to pray. Jesus' prayer had a twofold motivation. He went off to spend time with his Abba, and to discern the next step of his ministry. Our love for God requires something similar.

In his book *Into the Silent Land,* Martin Laird describes the calming, centering, and nourishing effect the practice of contemplation has on prisoners. He describes a young man who cuts himself with a sharp knife to dull emotional pain. "As long as I can remember," he says, "I have had this hurt inside.... I cut or burn myself so that the pain will be in a different place and on the outside." After learning how to pray the Jesus Prayer ("Jesus, Son of David, have mercy on me, a sinner") and practicing it twice a day for several weeks, the prisoner spoke movingly of what he had learned.

> I just want you to know that after only a few weeks of meditating half an hour in the morning and at night, the pain is not so bad, and for the first time in my life, I can see a tiny spark of something within myself that I can like.[31]

Laird notes that the spiritual liberation of which these prisoners speak is not something they acquired. The clear sense of their testimony is that they *discovered* rather than *acquired* the "sacred within."[32] Laird's point is that we are made for contemplation. Communion with God in the silence of the heart is a God-given capacity. Not to take quiet time for "the one thing necessary" (Luke 10:42) is to deny ourselves a relationship with a self-giving God who wants to love us into life.

A favorite line from the children's story *The Little Prince* comes to mind: "It is the time that you have wasted on the rose that makes the rose so important." Most of us don't like to waste time. We want the minutes, the hours of our day to be meaningful and productive. Yet if we won't spend time with those we love, those relationships will slowly deteriorate from lack of nourishment. The same is true with our relationship with God. We need to "waste" time with God in prayer if we want God to be at the center of our lives. One woman writes,

> My personal prayer time is certainly less structured. It happens in daily walks in the neighborhood, or on Saturday morning at Santa Monica beach or on visits to Huntington Park. The ocean speaks to me of God's presence as does the quiet time and space it grants me.[33]

We take time to pray not only to fall more deeply in love with God, but also to internalize God's way of viewing our lives, our joys and difficulties, the attachment/separation polarity of our lives. Kathleen Norris describes how the liturgy of the hours became a constant companion helping her cope with the difficulty of her husband's illness and death. She describes going to visit him in the hospital on a day when the air was so frigid that it hurt to breathe:

> As I cursed the cold and the icy pavement under my feet, these words of a canticle from the Sunday divine office came to mind:
>
> > Bless the Lord, winter cold and summer heat
> > Bless the Lord, dews and falling snow
> > Bless the Lord, nights and days
> > Bless the Lord, light and darkness
> > Bless the Lord, ice and cold
> > Bless the Lord, frosts and snows;
> > Sing praise to him and highly exalt him forever.
> > (Daniel 3:45–50)
>
> Unaccountably consoled, I was grateful that without my willing it, or being aware of how it happened, the liturgy of the hours I had prayed was having the desired effect. The words were now a part of me, and when I most needed them, the rhythms of my walking had stirred them up to erode my anxiety and self-pity, and remind me that blessings may be found in all things.[34]

Our Scripture and tradition provide countless passages and rituals that, internalized over time, become a part of us. They remind us who we are and whose pattern of life we are following. They enable us to live more intentionally in the rhythm of the liturgical year, thereby putting on the mind and heart of God so that we see as God sees and love as God loves in all the ups and downs of daily life. From the perspective of our faith, the attachment/separation tension is rooted in a theology of communion which finds expression in the community of memory we call the church.

In this chapter we have explored the challenges, tasks, and satisfactions of middle life through the major polarities and tensions in the individual and society. We do not aim to overcome these tensions— they are our source of growth—but rather we are invited, in each season of life, to find new ways of being young/old, destructive/creative, masculine/feminine, attached/separated. We also explored ways of doing theology that help us interpret the polarities within the context of an intentional faith.

We have seen that the young/old polarity needs to be nourished by a childlike faith that trusts God to love us into the women God empowers us to become through all the ups and downs, successes and failure of each season of life.

The destruction/creation polarity invites us to reflect on a theology of sin and grace. A theology of sin reminds us that we can never look at our brokenness or the brokenness of our world outside the context of God's mercy and compassion. A theology of grace challenges us to find God in every circumstance of our lives. The difficulties as well as the successes remind us, in the closing words of George Bernanos's novel *The Diary of a Country Priest:* "Tout est grâce"—All is grace.

The masculine/feminine polarity alerts us to the dignity of Christian personhood and the implications of being created in the image and likeness of God. It reminds us that the meaning we bring to male and female, masculine and feminine affirms or denies the full personhood of women and men.

Finally, the attachment/separation polarity points us toward a theology of communion. In an age of rampant, self-reliant individualism, a theology of communion reminds us of the need for healthy attachment in all areas of our lives—not only in our personal lives, but in our communal lives as well. In a culture that promotes individual spirituality apart from community, it is well to remember the importance of the community of memory called the church. Here we meet the Trinity—the Father/Mother, Jesus, and Holy Spirit of our tradition, the mystery of persons in communion—who continually calls us to live in God's name and work to humanize our world according to divine/human values. The activity of attachment needs the nourishment of separation. Not the separation of isolation, but the ability to go apart to nourish our inner lives through our relationship with God through prayer and creativity, reflection and action. The experience of God in each of the four polarities of life makes us more human. As we become more human, we become images of God.

FOOD FOR THOUGHT

1. How do you think our culture views middle-aged women today? Give specific examples.
2. What do you find most challenging about growing older gracefully?
3. In the presence of a loving and forgiving God, can you look back on your life and forgive those who have hurt and disappointed you? Can you forgive yourself for the hurts and disappointments you have caused others?
4. How do the drive toward autonomy and the drive toward relationality find expression in your life? What is the favorable ratio between them? Are you comfortable with these drives, or do you need to work toward a better balance between them?
5. Which of the three approaches to a Christian understanding of person—dualistic, complementary, egalitarian—resonates with your experience and why? How do you balance taking time to nourish your personal relationship with God with finding God in all the encounters and activities of your day?

REFLECTION

Let nothing trouble you,
Let nothing scare you,
All is fleeting,
God alone is unchanging,
Patience
Everything obtains.
Who possesses God
Nothing wants
God alone suffices.[35]

—Teresa of Avila

PRAYER

My soul magnifies the Lord,
   And my spirit rejoices in God my Savior,
For he has looked with favor on the lowliness of his servant.
   Surely, from now on all generations will call me blessed;
For the Mighty One has done great things for me,
   And holy is his name.

Luke 1:46–49

CHAPTER FOUR

• THE WINTER OF LIFE: TRUSTFUL FAITH •

Partaking wisdom, I have been given
The sum of many difficult acts of grace,
A vital fervor disciplined to patience.
This cup holds grief and balm in equal measure
Light, darkness. Who drinks from it must change.
Yet I am lavish with riches made from loss.[1]
—May Sarton

This poem by May Sarton describes the mixture of feelings women have shared with me about the season of winter in their lives. These years, beginning with age sixty-five, hold for every woman "grief and balm in equal measure." Well, almost "equal measure." For many women there seems to be more grief than balm. And yet when asked to share images of this wintry season, a mixture of sentiments emerge. On the one hand: biting, bleak, chilly, cutting, desolate, dismal, barren, frigid, harsh, fearful, raw, brittle. On the other hand: peaceful, calm, clear, stark, vital, still, tranquil, brilliant sun, smooth ice, slippery slope. Winter holds the promise of darkness and of light.

As we have seen in our discussion of previous seasons, the way in which women handle the "many difficult acts of grace" often depends upon what went before. We begin this chapter by reflecting on the tasks, challenges, and satisfactions of this winter season of life. We follow with

81

a consideration of the texture of faith that guides us through the light
and darkness of these years.

Until recently there has not been an abundance of research on this
phase of women's lives. At one recent conference on this topic, a seventy-year-old woman exclaimed, "There isn't anything about me, about
my stage of life in Dr. Levinson's chart!"[2] I acknowledged that this was
true. Levinson wanted to focus his study on young and middle adulthood. It is also worth noting that most of the theories on late adult
development are written by women and men in their middle years who
had little capacity for imagining themselves in the final season of life.
Now that these very individuals have entered their senior years, more
research and writing is being done by them and others on this final
stage of life.

Psychologist Erik Erikson makes a distinction between "elite elders" and "masses of elderly." The term "elite elders" refers to the few
women and men who, decades ago, quietly lived longer than others.
Their survival was viewed as a divine gift and their wisdom important
to the community. Now we have a large and reasonably healthy group
of elders. Unfortunately, modern culture has little to offer women and
men in their sixties and beyond. Erikson correctly maintains that the
role of aging needs to be reobserved and rethought in Western culture.[3]

A few decades ago, social scientists made a distinction between the
"young-old" (younger than seventy-five) and the "old-old" (older than
seventy-five). This distinction now seems outdated as the Census
Bureau projects that the eighty-five-and-older population will exceed
thirteen million by 2040. We have many women and men living longer,
in good health with many more productive years ahead of them.

As we saw in chapter three, Erikson describes generativity vs. stagnation as the task of middle adulthood. As an attribute of wisdom in
older people, Erikson claims that generativity has two faces. One is *car-
itas,* a Latin word for "charity," which Erikson takes in the broad sense
of caring for others. The other is *agape,* a Greek word for "love," which

he defines as a kind of empathy. Generative involvement, Erikson states, "involves taking care to pass on to the next generation what you've contributed to life."[4] At this state of life, one such expression of generativity can be seen in those women and men who contribute to the guidance of today's children, helping them to become adults in whose hands the world will be safe.

Erikson points out that some people seem old at forty because they resist personal growth and adventure. Others are youthful at seventy, filled with a zest for life and involved in various activities. A ninety-three-year-old priest is one of the most revered spiritual directors of our diocese. An eighty-five-year-old religious sister is a frequent speaker at national and diocesan functions. People are hungry for her wisdom and insight into the spiritual life. These individuals model how to grow older with dignity, grace, and continued vital involvement in the community they have served for years.

Many women and men over sixty-five years of age continue to be involved in leadership positions in a variety of fields—business, medicine, teaching, nursing, the arts—to name just a few. Many others continue productive and meaningful lives in occupations that do not demand mandatory retirement. As one sixty-two-year-old woman in a leadership position at a prominent hospital emphatically remarked, "I do not want the final phase of my life defined by loss and grief. I still have memories to make, thank you very much!"[5]

Making Memories

What are some of the memories to be made? In her book, *The Next Fifty Years*, psychotherapist Pamela Blair describes her grandmother as one who made memories until she died at the ripe young age of 101!

> As she aged, I watched her seek ways to grow intellectually (she loved U.S. history, listening to books on tape when she could no longer see well enough to read) and socially (in her seventies she had a boyfriend who was in his sixties!).

She walked everywhere and dressed with class. She enjoyed poli-
tics, creative pursuits, saving money to buy quality items, teaching
and playing with her grandchildren. In Grandma, I had a solid,
healthy vision of aging.[6]

Here is a woman whose upbeat attitude toward life, and above all, good
health, enabled her to continually find ways to stay energetically
involved with family, friends, and community. Another eighty-year-old
woman remembers her own mother, "My mother was eighty years old
and when she planted an apple tree and said, 'In five years we'll have
apples.'" This woman, now in her eighties herself, has always believed
in living each day to the fullest, without worry about what may or may
not be possible tomorrow. She recently enrolled in a community college
course in sign language. She explains, "In a few more semesters I'll be
fluent. Then I'll be able to go to the museum and persuade them to provide tours in sign language, for deaf art lovers."[7] Once again, we witness
a woman who lives in the present making meaningful memories!

Memories are still to be made in our family life. Many women rel-
ish and savor the joys and blessings of parenthood. One sixty-four-
year-old woman writes,

As a mother and a professional, balancing my time has been very
challenging and now the time has come for me to reflect and find
time to focus more on myself. Through the years I have found that
I've dedicated myself to the purpose of inspiring my children with
the highest ideals of character, conduct and patriotism. Now observ-
ing and seeing my five wonderful grown children, I am so proud of
them and the joy of my seven grandchildren is truly a great blessing.[8]

As we become less involved in the activities of our children and the
fast-paced world of work, we not only have more time for ourselves, but
also time to appreciate our partner's gifts, explore mutual interests, and
make each other a priority. One woman writes, "I want to make time to
form a better relationship with my husband who was always too busy."[9]

Another reflects, "As I detach myself from our adult children, I have elected to grow in my appreciation of my husband and our marriage. It takes work, but it is worth it."[10] Marriage in our final phase of life can grow yet further in intensity and communion. Common intellectual, artistic, leisure, and spiritual interests keep us mutually interested and engaged; support of each other in pursuit of diverse, individual interests is essential to the vitality of both. Wordless communion in one another's presence provides a deep sense of peace and contentment.

Making memories in our family life is influenced by how we feel about retirement. As many of us know, retirement can be a mixed blessing depending upon whether we are forced into it or choose it. Many of us may be startled to learn that the concept of the "golden years" originated as a public-relations program designed to make sixty-somethings feel good about their forced ousting from the workplace. Psychotherapist Pamela Blair asserts, "retirement isn't a natural part of the human life cycle"[11] because none of us, at any age, should be forced to think of ourselves as no longer a contributing member of society. However, since retirement is built in to the fabric of modern life, we need to develop a positive attitude toward it. Rather than think of it as "retiring" from life, why not think of it as turning our attention, energy, and enthusiasm to other ways of investing ourselves in life?

For many of us, retirement provides the opportunity to make memories of a different kind. Actress Helen Hayes writes, "I think the term 'retirement' is much too negative…. 'recreatement' sounds much more encouraging for the last and best third of one's life, which can be filled with newness."[12] Many "recreators" are involved in volunteer work at parishes, local hospitals, soup kitchens, or nonprofit organizations, which, without their assistance, could not continue their mission. One woman writes,

> After retirement, if I am physically able, I intend to stay alive my whole life. My mother did and so did my father. What I mean is that they were engaged in life. My mother entered into the life of her

grandchildren more vigorously than she entered into our lives. My father finished a novel that he had placed on the back burner for years. I'm going to go to the nearest preschool and say, "You have just acquired a resident grandmother. I'm going to be here a couple of days each week. I love children and want to stay involved with them." In this case, good modeling and a positive attitude toward retirement has truly paid off.[13]

Whether we are single, widowed, or married, our lives are enriched by the making of memories with our women friends. One woman speaks for many when she states:

> I don't know what would become of me if it weren't for the company
> of other women in my life. Women who are older offer me glimpses
> of what life can be in later years. Younger women offer an opportu-
> nity to share some of my hard-won wisdom and keep me in the
> swing of things. Last, and most importantly, the women who are in
> my age group, who are moving through the journey with me, are my
> comforters, my jovial companions, and my confidants.[14]

Research shows that women who have strong friendships with other women are healthier and live longer than those who lack them.[15]

Grandparents can play a vital role in the quality of memories their grandchildren have about growing up. An AARP study states that despite busy lives and geographic separation, grandparents are close to their grandchildren. In the best situations, grandparents become models for meeting life's problems with grace, wisdom, and courage. Many see their role as mentors, companions, advocates, or confidantes. Grandparents are important sources of unconditional love, comfort, and stability. Moreover, the genuine faith and wisdom of our grandparents can have a profound effect on the future attitudes of the young toward living a spiritual life. Spiritual writer Charles Fahey observes, "If older people view life, with its limitations and with its heartaches, within a spiritual context and with enthusiasm, then they are giving a kind of witness to the validity of religious thought that no younger person could ever give."[16] A grandmother confirms this truth, "One of the most important challenges of this time of my life is being a good example for my grandchildren, so that I might inspire them by my example of a faithful, loving Christian."[17]

Engagement in the humanization of the world is another source of memory-making. In her work with the poor in India, Mother Teresa and New Yorker Dorothy Day of the Catholic Worker Movement illustrate the tremendous good women accomplish through their dedication to the well-being of others through peace-making, a faith that does justice, and compassionate care for the poorest of the poor. James Martin writes of Dorothy Day,

> In 1973, at the age of seventy-six, Dorothy was arrested and jailed for her participation in the United Farm Workers rally supporting Cesar Chavez and the rights of migrant workers. A striking black-and-white photograph taken that day shows a birdlike, gray-haired woman wearing a secondhand dress and sitting on a folding chair. Dorothy gazes up calmly at two burly police officers, armed, who towered over her. It is a portrait of a lifetime of commitment, the dignity of discipleship and the absolute rightness of the gospel.[18]

A final way to make memories has to do with the development of our inner lives; that is, to take stock of who we have become in relation to self, others, and God. Taking the time to *be* as well as do—to read, reflect, enjoy more leisure activities—is to give ourselves the space to nurture and deepen our spiritual lives and to become our most authentic selves—a precious gift we have to return to God. A woman in her late sixties writes, "I feel my spirituality as of now is in an open, relaxed state. I no longer have to worry about kids, car pools, etc., so I can 'open' my life to really 'let God in'—feel God's presence, try to listen for His direction—really a good feeling—about my life because I really *feel* God."[19] Another woman agrees,

I consider myself to be extremely fortunate since retirement. I can attend daily liturgy and am inspired by my community to do so. My faith has deepened and I can accept my living alone in a much better way. I try to be a comfort to others and a source of help in other ways. I'm satisfied to be alone now and can grow spiritually daily.[20]

Losses and Diminishment

Making good memories in this final season of life does not mean that there will not be rough spots. Certainly one of the most obvious yet difficult experiences is the reality of loss. Loss of parents, husband or wife, brothers and sisters, friends, good looks, financial resources, loss of control over one's life, loss of good health, loss of a life's project that we gave our heart and soul to—all these experiences bring deep sadness and suffering into our lives. One woman describes a four-year grieving process during which she lost two brothers and one sister to cancer: "I have a huge hole in my heart. In the space of a couple years, all my brothers and my sister are gone. I feel so alone."[21]

This experience came home personally to me this year when my older sister, Kitty, died of brain cancer. She was a young sixty-eight year old. Kitty made it very clear to all of us that she wasn't interested in meeting God or seeing our deceased mother and father. She wanted to stay right here with her husband, six daughters, and her beloved grandchildren. I admired her honesty; she expressed what many of us feel, but would never admit.

Kitty is the first of my eight brothers and sisters to die. The death of a sibling hits home in a different way than the death of a parent, aunt or uncle—those of the older generation. Kitty is *my* generation. Her death during her still-vibrant years reminds me of the fragility and preciousness of life. I don't want to miss a moment of the gift we have been given.

A second area of difficulty for many of us is becoming dependent upon our children, other relatives, or the staff at a senior resident facility. This kind of dependence takes many forms. A woman falls and breaks her hip. She has lived independently but now must move in with her daughter or enter a senior residence. "I feel like such a burden. I try to stay out of the way as much as I can."[22] For another it was losing her vision which resulted in having to give up driving her car. "That was the worst," she expressed to me. "I lost my independence; my ability to go where I wanted, when I wanted. Now I have to wait upon others."[23]

Another area of worry for many senior adults is the possibility of living in a senior residency. In past agrarian cultures, where many generations lived together, the elderly were often a source of wisdom, stability, and comfort within the home. Relationships between grandparents and children in particular were a key source of meaning, joy, and satisfaction. Today our industrialized, technological, fast-paced urban life—where both parents often work and a diversity of family lifestyles have emerged—makes it very difficult to care for senior parents within the home. Many go into senior residencies willingly and create a life for themselves with their peers. One woman, Bertha, writes,

> At 67, I'm selfish enough to want my own way. I want to be with my own generation, people who understand the issues I live with.... Living with my children would have been a burden on me and on them. So I live in a home with lots of people my age.[24]

Others resent being "shelved" by their children and spend the rest of their lives bitter and resentful of their lot.

For many, it is not fear of death—we have made our peace with that. It is the dying process—the pain, the diminishment physically and mentally—that causes us the most anxiety and dread. One gentleman speaks for many of us when he writes,

> I think about death, but not enough to worry me. My views on religion have not changed in this sense. I do not believe necessarily in a burning hell, nor in a place in heaven where you fly around and wear crowns. That would bore me to death. It isn't like me. But I have faith enough to believe that God has taken care of me through all these

years. In all the ups and downs, struggle and strife, he must have been with me. Had to be. I could not make it by myself. If I trusted him while I was living, I would trust him with my soul. I am in accord with what God would do with me. I am not afraid of death. I am afraid of pain.[25]

This man's deep faith and trust keeps him honest, realistic, yet hope filled. For the elderly poor, life can be particularly anxiety-ridden as they are isolated in grim living conditions, lack transportation or money for shopping, suffer physical disabilities, and fear street crime. Community outreach to care for the elderly who can no longer care for themselves is a sign of a true Christian commitment to live the gospel.

Each one of us can contribute a story or a personal experience that expresses our fears and anxieties about these real diminishments of life. The key question is: Can these losses and diminishments of aging become thresholds for spiritual growth? Seen within the context of an intentional faith that trusts God is with us, these experiences can become the catalysts for growth in greater freedom, wisdom, and self-giving love.

Integrity vs. Despair

While contending with these challenging dimensions of aging, Erik Erikson maintains that the major task of this final stage of life is what he calls "consolidation of life." This final period brings together the conflicts, challenges, and satisfactions of a life of triumphs and disappointments. The task involves a struggle between two polar opposites that take center stage at this time of life: Integrity vs. Despair.

"Integrity" involves the acknowledgement that we are responsible for our own lives. This includes the acceptance of "our one and only life cycle, and the people who have become significant in it, as something that had to be and that, by necessity, permitted no substitutions."[26] One seventy-five-year-old woman writes, "I find this a time of acceptance, a peaceful acceptance, 90 percent of the time. Ten percent of the time I still ask 'why'; I search for understanding of what has gone before."[27]

"Despair" expresses the realization that time is short, too short to attempt another life or alternate roads to integrity. Erikson states, "In old age...the struggle is between a sense of one's own integrity and a feeling of defeat, of despair about one's life in the phase of normal physical disintegration. The fruit of that struggle is wisdom."[28] Erikson contends that real wisdom comes from life experience, well digested. It involves living in the present, while circling back to see how the lessons learned in each season of life have ripened into the wisdom of old age. To grow older, however, does not automatically bring wisdom. Erikson writes, "When we looked at the life cycle in our forties, we looked to old people for wisdom. At eighty, though, we look at other eighty-year-olds to see who got wise and who not. Lots of old people don't get wise, but you don't get wise unless you age."[29]

The circling back to attain wisdom regarding one's one and only life involves living in the present as we journey back to acknowledge and take responsibility of the successes and disappointments of our lives. This involves honesty, humility, and, most important, the ability to forgive ourselves and others. The challenge is to view those who have hurt us from the perspective of compassion and forgiveness. In addition, can we acknowledge our own guilt, sadness, and remorse for the hurt we have caused others and even ourselves and ask for forgiveness? To do so is to allow the psyche to heal, and to accept our lives for what they have been—a mixture of triumphs and disappointments, successes and failures.

Needless to say, women and men who believe in a compassionate and forgiving God who rejoices in our successes, heals our memories, and brings victory out of our defeats, come through this struggle with the balance favoring integrity over despair. In a recent *Newsweek* interview, as he reflects on his twilight years, evangelist Billy Graham illustrates this "consolidation of life" as he takes comfort in a loving God:

I think about heaven a great deal, I think about the failures in my life in the past, but know that they have been covered by the blood of Christ, and that gives me a great sense of confidence. I have a certainty about eternity that is a wonderful thing, and I thank God for giving me that certainty. I do not fear death. I may fear a little bit about the process, but not death itself, because I think the moment that my spirit leaves this body, I will be in the presence of the Lord.[30]

Trustful Faith

Billy Graham expresses the trusting faith we need to guide us through this season of our lives. It is a faith which believes God will be true to God's promise to be with us in all things: memory-making, losses and diminishments, and consolidating our lives in a choice for integrity over despair. Many women in the winter of life experience a deep peace that comes from looking back on former seasons of their life and realizing that through God's guidance and fidelity, they have negotiated the seasons well and have attained spiritual wisdom. They continue to live this season with enthusiasm and vitality. One woman in her sixties reflects,

> My spiritual journey has become deeper and more active....I have realized of late that all of my life is a spiritual journey and that what I thought was merely talking to God was indeed a form of prayer. I know that my journey now is taking me into a deeper realization of the need to trust God and to relinquish my grip....to let go of control, I suppose. It was a wonderful realization to know that God chose me, not the other way around....Finally, I have come to the wonderful realization that God loves me no matter how I fail and wants only what is good for me. It is, however, still up to me to make the decisions using the gifts God has given me.[31]

While this woman expresses gratitude in the realization that God loves her no matter what, a seventy-year-old wife, mother, and grandmother appreciates God's fidelity through her struggle to mature:

I think that trust is a good word to describe it. But I was a *long* time coming to that. My faith and my personality were *very* immature until past forty-five. You described the "happy housewife" who suddenly reached a midlife crisis and found that she wanted a career. I was the reverse—an "unhappy housewife," hating scrubbing floors and cooking and wanting a career. Then suddenly I found that was not really what I wanted. And then I began to grow.[32]

This honest woman illustrates for us a theme that we have returned to many times throughout this book—God comes to us in our personal history as we are and where we are. While there are guides to point the way, there is no set timetable for growth toward human and spiritual maturity. We are each unique and God's guidance in our lives is tailor-made according to our personalities and life circumstances.

As a context within which to grow spiritually in a trusting faith during this wintry season of life, I share with you the guidance of two mystics of our tradition. As I stated in the introduction of this book, one of my goals is to introduce (or reintroduce) you to mystics of our tradition who have something to say to us about finding God in our life experience. When I struggled for life in my own battle with cancer, I gained sustenance from both these friends of God in different ways. I hope they can be helpful to you as well. First, the life and writings of Teresa of Avila remind us that we are invited to fall more deeply in love with God as the goal of our journey through each season of our lives. Second, the dark night of the spirit of John of the Cross calls attention to the truth we often forget—God is with us in the struggles and difficulties of life to help us choose life, to choose God, even when we don't feel God with us.

Teresa of Avila's Spiritual Journey

Teresa of Avila was a sixteenth-century Carmelite nun whose relationship with Jesus changed her life. She is a source of encouragement to many of us. She experienced a midlife conversion at age thirty-nine and, at sixty-two, began writing her most important work on prayer, *The Interior Castle*. On September 27, 1970, Teresa was named the first woman doctor of the church. Since this title had been bestowed only on men, most theologians did not think a woman would ever receive it. Teresa was honored with this title because it is eminently clear to anyone who reads her writings, that her knowledge and wisdom were inspired by God's presence to her, even though she lacked formal education.

The *Interior Castle* is a spiritual classic with meaning not only for sixteenth-century Catholics but for every generation of Christians who endeavor to live an intentional spiritual life. Some of us may not be attracted to Teresa's images or her style of writing as a woman of the sixteenth century. Her call to "leave the world" to pursue union with God as a Carmelite nun places her in a monastic setting that is very different from our own. A spirituality for our time must be incarnational; that is, one that guides busy women and men to find God precisely in the world in which we live and work. Yet Teresa's insights into the spiritual journey are full of wisdom especially for those of us in the final season of our lives. She provides us with a way to stay connected to God as the center out of which all our concerns, struggles, and activities proceed and are attended to. In particular, Teresa describes for us a relationship with God that in many ways follows the same dynamics of our human relationships, evolving through stages from acquaintance, to friendliness, then on to friendship, love and finally, union. Just as personal relationships have their ups and downs, peaks and valleys, periods of intimacy as well as times of staleness, so too does our relationship with God. Most important, the degree to which we are willing to risk vulnerability to intimacy in our human relationships provides some indication of our willingness to risk the possibility of intimacy with God.

Many of us don't realize that this call to intimacy with God is possible, or that we are good enough or holy enough for God to love us in this personal way. Yet the Scriptures remind us over and over again that

God's love is not earned; it is a gift. In her book on spiritual direction, Sister Janet Ruffing shares a reflection from one of her directees that describes this relationship. In the account that follows, this person shows an awareness of the way Christ lives in him, acts in him, and is one love with him:

> Paul writes, is it cold? I have Christ with me. Is it hot? I have Christ with me. Am I sick? I have Christ with me.... What Paul is really saying is if you are really God-connected...let it snow...let it rain, let the sun shine.... whatever it is, I have that center. I have that constant connection with my beloved no matter what. I feel that I've always been called...it's a love affair. If it isn't that, it is nothing. Jesus is love, God is love. St. John writes that over and over again. Sometimes I've been so angry at the church for not being able to do a better PR job on selling love. I feel that somehow God has been short-changed because we really don't preach that this is pure loving. It's a love that is so freeing because real love wants growth and permits growth.... Divine love wants to nurture you and wants you to grow in the face of the divine person. So divine love is...to be kissed by God.[33]

Not all of us experience Jesus as passionately as this young man describes. Others describe their experience of God more as a quiet, loving attentiveness to God within the core of their being as well as to the people and activities of their day. Teresa is certain, however, that all of us are called to experience this God-connection. Teresa describes the soul as a beautiful interior castle made of diamonds or crystal with seven inner dwelling places, which contain many rooms. The meaning Teresa assigns to the word *soul* does not oppose soul to body. Rather she uses the term to point to the deepest and most mysterious aspects of the person being acted upon directly by God.

As she describes individual rooms in this castle, Teresa seems to suggest that they are like concentric circles, gradually leading into a single chamber, the center of the soul where God dwells. As we journey

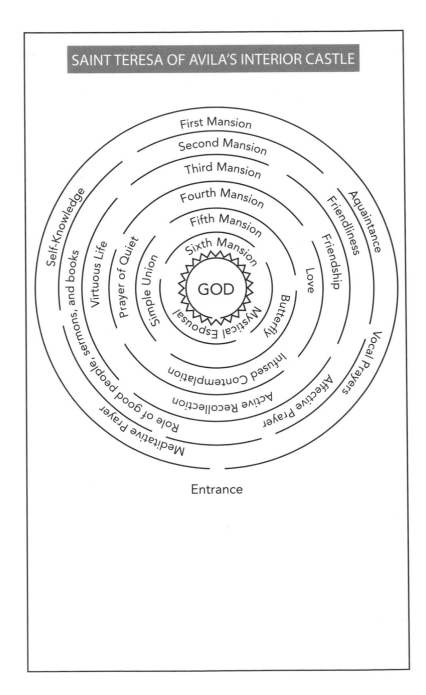

SAINT TERESA OF AVILA'S INTERIOR CASTLE

First Mansion
Second Mansion
Third Mansion
Fourth Mansion
Fifth Mansion
Sixth Mansion
GOD

Self-Knowledge
Virtuous Life
Prayer of Quiet
Simple Union
Mystical Espousal
Butterfly
Love
Friendship
Friendliness
Aquaintance

sermons, and books
Role of good people,
Meditative Prayer
Active Recollection
Infused Contemplation
Affective Prayer
Vocal Prayers

Entrance

through the different mansions, we are invited to arrive at a more authentic knowledge of self and the God who dwells in the center of the castle. The more intentional we become about living a life of union with God, the more our service of others will become effective and fruitful.

The idea of the soul consisting of mansions or dwelling places comes from the Gospel of John. Christ says, "Do not let your hearts be troubled. Believe in God, believe also in me. In my Father's house there are many dwelling places.... I go to prepare a place for you" (John 14:1–2). Teresa invites us to begin the journey into the depths of the center of our own interiority through the gateway of prayer. "Mental prayer in my opinion," she says, "is nothing else than an intimate sharing between friends. It means taking the time frequently to be alone with Him who we know loves us."[34]

There are many people who never make it into the castle. They are lost but don't know they are lost. They are so preoccupied with the pleasures of life that they have no time or need for a spiritual life. Once in the castle (which Teresa describes as no small accomplishment in itself), she describes the journey as an internal progression of seven stages leading to union with God.

A brief overview of the mansions provides us with the opportunity to circle back and connect with the response of faith that I have described in each season of life. The first two mansions describe faith as *Personal Relationship*. The first mansion involves waking up to the importance of the spiritual life. Teresa tells us that the soul knocks at the gateway to the castle to seek entrance through vocal prayer, meditation on Jesus in the Gospels, and religious services.

> For the most part, God remains outside of us. We have not heard or understood the call to turn inward and find God within our deepest selves. Many "reptiles" (things of the world to which we are overly attached) also try to get in. Many of them do.[35]

In the second mansion we begin to hear God inviting us into a more personal relationship. We realize we have to listen more carefully to how God is speaking to us through liturgy, sacraments, and the circumstances of our lives. We also recognize that we need to bring external behaviors, activities, attitudes, and desires into agreement with the invitation to "come, follow me." We make more effort to pray, to spend time in meditation, which means thinking about Jesus' life and his values so as to put on his mind and heart. We can't love someone we don't know. Teresa points out that God uses intermediaries such as sermons, conversations with good people, inspiring books and trials to call us more deeply into friendship with him. One woman in her forties describes this stage. "I have not yet met the Lord. I rely on intermediaries like good friends, books that are recommended to me, maybe...someday."[36] Teresa speaks about the need for good friends, especially those who will be honest with us:

> Love such persons as much as you like. There can be very few of them.... When one of you is striving after perfection, she will at once be told that she has no need to know such people—that it is enough for her to have God. But to get to know God's friends is a very good way of "having" God, as I have discovered by experience, it is most helpful. For, under the Lord, I owe it to such persons that I am not in hell.[37]

For all of us, friends are a lifeline who mediate God's presence to us through their support, encouragement, and when necessary, honest feedback. The third mansion describes what I presented in chapter two as *Reflective Faith*. Here Teresa paints a portrait of the good Christian many of us have striven hard to become. We feel that we have answered the question: Who is God *for me?* We pray regularly, celebrate liturgy weekly, try to live a virtuous life, and extend ourselves in service to others. Our prayer has become more personal and affective. Teresa comments, "This is a state to be desired."[38] Two women provide contemporary descriptions of these mansions:

I consider myself a good Christian. I am currently trying to deepen my relationship with God. I do the outward things—liturgy, adoration, prayer but I struggle with how to deepen my prayer. How do I keep my mind from wandering? How do I enter into continuous conversation with God that I read about? How do I find God in all things?[39]

This woman is struggling to find God not only in her prayer life, but in the continuous conversation with God that can take place throughout the day. Another woman writes,

I'm searching for more inner peace with my faith. Trying to grow beyond what was taught during my twelve years of Catholic education and beyond my parents' beliefs. I want my faith to be simple, comfortable and very special to me and not for everyone else. I want to learn through faith, grace, courage, patience and humility what God's will is in my life—I love God very much![40]

Teresa tells us that God is pleased with our efforts to grow in friendship with him, but there is more. She calls our attention to the rich young man who was a good Jew, for he followed the commandments as he had been taught. But he wanted to know what more he could do. When Jesus invited him to leave all and follow him more closely, the young man went away sad, for he had many possessions (Matthew 19:16–22). Is the same true about us? Teresa cautions us: "There is need of still more in order that the soul possess the Lord completely. It is not enough to say we want it, just as it was not enough for the young man whom the Lord told what one must do in order to be perfect."[41] While there is no one-to-one correlation between chronological age and spiritual growth, the transition from the third to the fourth mansions often occurs at midlife. Teresa tells us that those in the third mansion eventually experience a disquiet, a restlessness. Neither prayer nor life satisfies as it did before. We may feel that we have lost our way. We no longer feel in control. One woman writes, "I do not seem to be in control of my life right now. It's like I'm at the wheel of a ship that is moving but I'm not the one who is really steering."[42] We sense that the faith, or our way of living it, that guided us through the first half of life won't be enough for the second half. Yet many good Christian women and men choose to stay in the third mansion. They become comfortable with their notion of God, their participation in the liturgical life of the church, and their effort to lead a good life. In the words of one woman, "I don't want anyone to rock my boat. I'm comfortable where I am."[43]

The fourth mansion represents the critical decision of autumn's *Intentional Faith.* We either enter into a deeper transformative relationship with God or realize that we are satisfied with equating religion with its codes, creeds, and rituals. One forty-one-year-old woman captures this experience when she writes,

> Life has changed greatly the last few years. Now I have opened the
> door and have let the Holy Spirit move into my very person....
> When I was a young seventeen- to twenty-five-year-old, faith was
> not as important to me. I am ready to open my soul and mind even
> more to the way of Christ and let the Holy Spirit take and show me
> the light—the path of life to walk.[44]

Teresa introduces the fourth mansion with a scriptural reference from Psalm 118:32: "when you have enlarged my heart." God now becomes more active; we become more passive, as God enlarges, expands, dilates, and stretches the soul so that we have the capacity to receive the fullness of the divine life more completely.[45] Any woman who has experienced vaginal delivery knows the experience of being dilated and stretched so as to bring forth new life. In many ways we are not in control of the process, yet we must cooperate with it so that new life can come forth. The same is true in our spiritual lives. We are invited to be open to the in-breaking of God in a new way. One woman expresses this invitation well:

I'm in transition again!!! With my children on their own, the question of meaning and purpose have resurfaced. My spirituality is changing and I'm struggling with letting God in deeper.[46]

In the fourth mansion, Teresa introduces us to the simple, loving awareness of what our tradition calls contemplative prayer. She explains that a person finds herself desiring solitude, and without much effort, involuntarily closes her eyes, because she feels God calling her to turn within and become aware of God's presence in the core of her being. Jesus invites us to such prayer in John's Gospel: "Abide in me as I abide in you…. Those who abide in me and I in them bear much fruit" (John 15:4–5). Teresa explains this experience in her own imaginative fashion:

> But one noticeably senses a gentle drawing inward, as anyone who goes through this will observe, for I don't know how to make it clearer. It seems to me that I have read where it was compared to a hedgehog curling up or a turtle drawing into its shell…. In the case of this recollection, it doesn't come when we want it, but when God wants to grant us this favor.[47]

Contemplation does not refer only to an inner attentiveness to God in times of prayer, but to a way of life that spills over into the whole fabric of our lives. We take our prayer into life, and bring our life into prayer. Our families, friends, the people who make up the culture of our work, are beginning to be seen through God's eyes rather than the self-centeredness of our own. We find ourselves better able to be present to people on their own terms, rather than try to recreate them in our image and likeness. We find ourselves freer, better able to go with the flow, to "let go and let God." We are more available, more responsive, and more grateful—dispositions especially helpful in dealing with the ups and downs, highs and lows of this final phase of our lives.

After this time of transition, the final three mansions describe growth in self-knowledge, an ever deepening union with God, and fruitful service in Jesus' name. The fifth and sixth mansions describe what I presented in chapter two as *Paradoxical Faith:* How can new life come out of death? In the fifth mansion, Teresa illustrates the paradoxical nature of faith at this time in our lives by reminding her sisters that they must die to the selfish self-centeredness and willfulness in their own lives rather than complain about such vices in others. She uses the image of a cocooned caterpillar that, in dying to its "ugly" self, becomes a butterfly, an image of our true selves. Here Teresa addresses what Jung described as the shadow side of our personality, and the importance of owning the negative parts of ourselves if we want to discover our true selves. Teresa writes,

> Oh, then, my daughters! Let us hasten to perform this task and spin this cocoon. Let us renounce our self-love and self-will, and our attachment to earthly things.... Let the silkworm die...let it die. Then finally, the worm, which is large and ugly, comes right out of the cocoon a beautiful butterfly.[48]

As we noted in chapter three, it is not attachments that block our spiritual growth, but rather *inordinate* attachments that make persons, places, or things ends in themselves. For Teresa, the asceticism that is necessary for the silkworm to die is the ability to move beyond personal self-interest in order to extend oneself, through compassion and charity toward others.

All too often in our tradition, asceticism has focused on disciplining the body, affectivity, and sexuality in ways that encourages a dualistic approach to life—spirit/good, body/bad. Teresa encourages us to think of asceticism in more relational terms: how do we respond to the daily challenges that living in community and interconnection with others pose? The sacrifices entailed in marital and family life, especially in the raising of children and/or caring for elderly parents; the daily grind of earning a living, decisions about the use and dispositions of goods; the chaste exercise of sexuality that is necessary in every vocation; our care for the earth—all these areas of our lives call us to de-center, making the well being of others our first concern.[49]

The sixth mansion describes Teresa's experience of what John of the Cross refers to as the dark night of the spirit. Severe illnesses, misunderstandings, seeming abandonment by friends and by God, which many of us endure in this season of life, can be experiences of the dark night of spirit. As we will see, God invites us to give over to God our intellect, memory, and will in a final surrender of our whole being to God. Teresa describes her experience in her own life, "For in this state, grace is so hidden that not even a very tiny spark is visible. The soul doesn't think it has any love of God or that it ever had any, for if it has done some good, or the good Lord has granted it some favor, all of this seems to have been dreamed up or fancied."[50]

The final, seventh mansion describes the fruits of a *Trusting Faith*. The image Teresa uses to describe the transforming union that takes place here between God and us is spiritual marriage. This image, so familiar to all of us, is one excellent way we have to explain the mystery of the total gift of one person to another. We have intimations of such a union in married couples who, in spending fifty or sixty plus years together, have transformed each other through their gift of love. The same is true in our relationship with God. Teresa states that the soul is made one with God in such a way that "just as those who are married cannot be separated, God doesn't want to be separated from the soul."[51] There is now a union of wills, a mutuality in love, a partnership between God and the individual person that is the source of great fruitfulness in every aspect of life. Teresa concludes,

> In sum, Sisters, what I conclude with is that we shouldn't build castles in the air. The Lord doesn't look so much at the greatness of our works as at the love with which they are done. And if we do what we can, His Majesty will enable us each day to do more and more."[52]

A mutual indwelling; a fruitful partnership. Like two people who cannot be separated, God makes us one with him so that the love that God has given us will, in turn, be shared with a world in such need of his presence.

Upon occasion, each of us needs a roadmap to get us from where we are to a particular destination. Teresa's gift to us is a map of the peaks and valleys that make up the terrain of the spiritual life. Full of practical wisdom, she also provides many suggestions as to how to maneuver our way through them to our final destination of union with God.

John of the Cross: Dark Night of the Spirit

For those of us whose lives seem to contain more "grief than balm," John of the Cross's dark night of the spirit may offer a helpful interpretative framework that complements Teresa's description of the spiritual journey to our true self in God. Chapter two related the agonizing experience which gave rise to John's writing on the dark night of the soul. But like Teresa, his concern is that we become free to respond to the gift of love offered us by God.

John identifies two movements within the dark night—the dark night of the senses and the dark night of the spirit. I described the dark night of the senses as an interpretative framework for understanding, from a faith perspective, the issues and challenges of midlife. This dark night takes place in the realm of our sense experience—sight, smell, touch, hearing, taste. This experience happens to many of us. Through it, and with our cooperation, God is rightly ordering our affectivity so that all our loves are rooted in God.

The dark night of the spirit takes place in the realm of intellect, memory, and will. John believes this dark night happens to fewer people and is much more difficult. However, since we now live longer, and as I listen to the experiences of women and men in the context of spiritual direction, I think this night of the spirit happens more often than we think. I believe John describes these two dark nights as happening sequentially for purposes of clarity, but in real life they normally overlap and intermingle.

Gerald May points out that when John speaks of the dark night he is not referring to something sinister, as in "powers of darkness" or "the dark side." The Spanish word that John used for *dark* is *oscura*, which means simply "obscure." In the same way that things are difficult to see at night, the deepest relationship between God and us is hidden from us. A contemporary Carmelite author, Sister Constance Fitzgerald, reminds us that the "dark night is not primarily *something*, an impersonal darkness like a difficult situation or distressful psychological condition, but *someone*, a presence leaving an indelible imprint on the human spirit and consequently one one's entire life."[53] The fact that it is God at work causes John to refer to the dark night as "happy," "glad," "guiding," and full of "absolute grace." The problem is that it doesn't feel happy, glad, or full of grace!

The dark night of the spirit refers to the process of emptying and freeing the spiritual faculties of intellect, memory, and will. Its purpose is to get down to the deepest roots of our attachments so as to free our spiritual powers to love more fully. It is not something God does to us, but a process that God does with us—a coparticipation between ourselves and God.

I find it helpful to think of the purification process of the dark night in the context of our most important human relationships. Over the journey of a lifetime, we have plenty of opportunities to learn to love selflessly and generously. But it is not automatic. We learn it through putting the well-being of others before our own. Such loving in everyday life demands a similar, deepening purification of those patterns of thinking, willing, acting that prevent us from loving others as we should. Such a process is ongoing throughout our lives. One possible explanation for our high divorce rates is that some men and women simply are not willing to work through the difficulties, tensions, and misunderstandings that test a marriage. Yet staying the course can open the way to deeper understanding, friendship, and commitment. John describes the dark night of the spirit: God divests the faculties, the affections, the senses both spiritual and sensory, interior and exterior. God leaves the intellect in darkness, the will in aridity and the memory in emptiness and the affections in supreme affliction.[54]

When John says the intellect is emptied and left in darkness, he is warning us that a time may come when what we thought we believed doesn't sustain us the way it has in the past. Sometimes people wonder if they have been "had." Is what I believed all my life about God, Jesus, life after death, really true? When Thérèse of Lisieux was sick with tuberculosis, she struggled with temptations against belief in God and the reality of heaven. She did not tell anyone for fear of scandalizing them. Later in her diary she describes this affliction:

> And now all of a sudden, the mists around me have become denser than ever; they sink deep into my soul and wrap it around so that I can't recover the deeper images of my native country anymore—everything has disappeared. I get tired of the darkness all around me, and try to refresh my jaded spirits with thoughts of that bright country where my hopes live; and what happens? It is worst torment ever; the darkness itself seems to borrow, from the sinners who lived in it, the gift of speech. I hear its mocking accents: It's all a dream, this talk of a heavenly country, bathed in light, scented with delicious perfumes, and of a God who made it all, who is to be your possession in eternity. You really believe, do you, that the mist which hangs about you will clear away later on? But death makes nonsense of your hopes; it will only mean a night darker than ever, a night of mere non-existence.[55]

What is happening here? Thérèse is faced with a choice to believe, to have faith, even when she does not feel it. Later she states, "I believe I have made more acts of faith in this past year than all through my whole life."[56]

In describing the purification of the memory, John speaks about a time when the imagination can no longer connect life's memories to produce meaning and hope. We look back over our lives and remember more of our disappointment and failures than our successes and triumphs. Was the effort we put forth for family, a life's project, worth it?

In the end what do we have to show for it? Erikson described this struggle as the choice of integrity over despair. An example of what I think this struggle looks like in the here and now is found in a memoir by Margaret Brennan, I.H.M., entitled *What Was There For Me Once.* Sister Margaret is a Servant of the Immaculate Heart of Mary—a community of religious women to whom I am very close who educated me from grade school through college. In this memoir, written at the age of eighty-three, Sister Margaret describes her love affair with the church from her childhood, through entrance into religious life, and then as a leader who guided religious communities through "the bright colors of Vatican II" to the "gift and grace of fewness" of religious life today.[57]

In a chapter entitled "Seeing Through Prayer," Brennan shares with her readers a retreat experience. She writes, "As I journeyed through the [spiritual] exercises once again, I looked long and hard at what retirement might mean for me and what it would ask of me. Two scripture passages became the heart of my reflections touching sensitive areas that will challenge me for the rest of my days."[58] The first is the story of Martha and Mary in Luke 11:1–4. Margaret tells us that a trap and temptation for her is to complain about the church and mourn over it—how it should or should not be, what it is doing or not doing. Jesus' words to the zealous but troubled Martha spoke to her: "Martha, Martha, you are worried and troubled over many things....but only one thing is necessary." The second passage is from John 21:18, which records the words of the Risen Jesus to Peter on the shore of the lake.

> I tell you most solemnly, when you were young, you put on your own belt and walked where you liked, but when you grow old you will stretch out your hands, and someone else will put a belt around you and take you where you would rather not go. Margaret asks the questions many of us ask as we face retirement and an unknown future: "Will I indeed be able to go where I would rather not? And will I even have a choice?"[59]

Brennan's years of leadership in religious life and in the church are behind her. The church she dedicated her life to has not become the church of her dreams. The religious life she loves so passionately is redefining itself from the many to the few.

I have interpreted Brennan's experience through the prism of the dark night of memory. She reviews her life—triumphs and setbacks— as a consolidation of its ultimate meaning. Instructive for us is her deep faith that compels her to bring her life experience under the guidance of the gospel. For a woman who is revered around the world for her commitment to the implementation of Vatican II and the renewal of religious life, the sharing of her "times of light and times of disappoint-ment" is a source of hope for many. She models for all of us the reality that one day we too will face the choice of whether or not to surrender the final meaning of our life's project into the hands of a loving God. The dark night of the will involves the final purification of our ability to love. However it happens in our lives, those we have loved and cher-ished as providing the meaning and context of our lives, seems to be cut off, taken away, or withdrawn. Here we find ourselves asking: Who will be there for me?

A concrete illustration of this experience is found in the decision to place a parent in a senior residency. One family that I am close to recently made this very difficult decision. It is hard on everyone, but particularly the mother who had lived independently for many years. Now she feels she has lived too long and is a burden on her children, who have abandoned her in a place she does not want to be. I hope that through her deep faith she will eventually adjust to her new way of liv-ing and make new friends that will help her find meaning and a sense of belonging in this final phase of her life.

What is the purification and transformation that is taking place here? As I have said before and will remind us all again, God never sends us suffering. Life brings it—all on its own. God's promise is to be with us, guiding us to greater freedom and a deeper, better love. John of the Cross describes our human powers of knowing, remembering, and

willing as deep caverns of feeling that have the capacity for the plenti-
tude of God. As long as these caverns are full of other things, we can't
genuinely ache for them to be filled with God. When we experience the
fragility of what or whom we have staked our lives on; when we experience the disappointment of our life project or our loved ones—only
then, says John, will we thirst and hunger and yearn for God to be the
fulfillment of our hearts' desires.

John's response to this experience of the dark night is illustrated for
us by Thérèse of Lisieux and Sister Brennan: their embrace of the theological virtues of faith, hope, and love. We are challenged to *choose* to
have faith in God for God's sake, hope in God for God's sake, and love
of God for God's love especially when we don't feel it.

The twelfth-century spiritual writer Bernard of Clairvaux wrote a
short treatise entitled "On Loving God," which explores through four
stages of loving the same journey that John describes. The first stage
describes love of self for self's sake. I doubt this stage needs any explanation. The second stage describes our love of God for self's sake. Here
we love God for what God does for us. Many people live their entire
lives in this stage. The third stage is the one John is describing as the
fruit of the dark night of the spirit: love of God for God's sake. Here
we find ourselves falling in love not with the consolations of God, but
with the God of consolations: the God of absolute mystery, incompre-
hensible love, the Beyond in our midst who wants only to love us into
life, to help us discover our true selves in God. The fourth stage is the
loving of self for God's sake.

While I have described this dark night of the spirit as an interpretative framework for the final phase of our lives, it can happen at other
times of our lives as well. God loves each of us uniquely and leads us
according to our personalities and life experiences.

What is the healing process of the dark night? Through the dark
night of the spirit, the virtue of faith opens our intellects to acknowledge the inadequacy of all our theological constructs for naming God.
Thus we are freer to allow God to lead us into newer, better ways of

knowing God. The virtue of hope heals our memory so we are able to give the totality of our lives—its successes and failures—into the forgiving, merciful hands of God. The virtue of love encourages us to love ourselves and others the way God has loved us—with infinite compassion, mercy, and forgiveness. Now we are better able to know, to hope, and to love from God's perspective. In the final stanza of John's poem we read about the depth of love God wants us to experience as the final goal of our journey.

> How gently and lovingly
> you wake in my heart
> Where in secret you dwell alone;
> And in your sweet breathing,
> Filled with good and glory,
> How tenderly you swell my
> heart with love.[60]

John of the Cross's dark night prepares us for the last stage of loving described by Bernard of Clairvaux—the love of self for God's sake. Here we begin to see ourselves as God sees us—as the beloved of God. I was amazed when I read the following selection from a seventy-seven-year-old woman, which expresses this final stage of loving so well:

> Years have mellowed me considerably so that I've come to be much more gentle and forgiving with myself and others because I've experienced a God who is so gentle, loving, forgiving, inviting and patient—an ever present God. I've found a God I can trust and who trusts me.
>
> The "beloved of God" in John's gospel has become a faith model for me: "Another man was sent from God, named the Beloved of God. The beloved was sent to be a witness to the light. The Beloved was not the light, but was a witness to the light."
>
> That is my relationship to God at this point in my life—to be a witness to the Light. To be this witness in joy and hope, in compassion and love in the midst of all my diminishment. I see God in many faces![61]

In this chapter we have reflected on the "grief and balm," "light and darkness" that make up this final phase of our lives. May Sarton ends the introductory poem to this chapter with the line, "Yet I am lavish with riches made from loss." We have looked at the riches made from loss through the eyes of a trusting faith. We have interpreted the memory-making, difficulties, and tasks of this stage of our lives through the interpretative frameworks of Teresa of Avila's *Interior Castle,* and John of the Cross's dark night of the spirit. Teresa reminds us that the goal of our lives humanly and spiritually is coming to know our true selves in God, so as to love others as God has loved us. She provides us with a map of this journey to God who dwells in the core of our being. John of the Cross encourages us to remember that through all the difficulties, disappointments, and suffering of life, God is enlarging our hearts so we have a greater capacity to receive him, to be transformed by him, and in turn share God's love with others. Both of them remind us that when all is said and done, we need to love God, others, and ourselves as best we can, and then leave the rest up to God.

FOOD FOR THOUGHT

1. How do you (or will you) continue to make memories during the winter of your life?
2. What experiences of loss and diminishment are particularly difficult for you? Have any of them been thresholds for spiritual growth?
3. Does Erikson's description of the tension of integrity vs. despair resonate with your life experience or the experience of others?
4. God's presence in your life encourages you to choose integrity. How do you do that? What blocks you from embracing integrity?
5. Teresa of Avila's *Interior Castle* describes what growth in friendship with God looks like as we journey through the stages of life. What does God say to you about your own relationship with the divine?
6. John of the Cross's dark night of the spirit is about learning to believe in God for God, hope in God for God, love God for God. Are you there yet? Can you pray for the desire to trust God in this way?

REFLECTION

Nothing is more practical than
Finding God,
That is, than *falling in love*
In a quite absolute, final way.
What you are in love with,
What seizes your imagination,
Will affect everything.
It will decide
What will get you out of bed
In the morning,
What you do with your evenings,
How you spend your weekends,
What you read, who you know,
What breaks your heart,
And what amazes you with joy and gratitude.
Fall in love, stay in love,
And it will decide everything.[62]

—attributed to Pedro Arrupe, S.J.

PRAYER

Father, in the end
The only cure for a weary heart
Is a renewing glimpse of your face
And a rebirth of passion.
I do not pray, therefore,
To finish the race
But for the heart to take the next step,
And the next,
And all that follow.[63]

—Hildegard of Bingen

CONCLUSION

We conclude our journey with the hope that several key themes will linger in your memory. First, this book has been about a theology of grace. Grace, the self-communication of God's very being to us, works from the inside out. God heals our way of thinking, feeling, and acting so that we become our true selves in God.

Second, God comes to us in our personal history, with our particular life circumstances, personalities, strengths, and limitations. The circumstances of our lives influence us but they don't determine us. God is the potter who works with us, molding and forming us into the unique women we are called to be: "The glory of God is the human person fully alive." Third, developmental psychologists speak about a "will to health" that is built into the fabric of our being. I think of this truth every time I see slabs of cement and wonder how those tiny blades of grass found a crack through which to grow and turn toward the sun. The same is true for us. We have a will to health within us—the Holy Spirit joins our spirit—moving us to health, wholeness, and holiness through all the successes, challenges, and disappointments of our lives as the final goal of our journey to God. Finally, there is a unity to our love for God and our love of neighbor. The more we grow in our relationship with God, the freer we are to love others as God has loved us. I close with a quote from a favorite professor that summarizes the main theme of this book. It says it all:

> The experience of grace is both divinizing and humanizing.
> Grace makes us like God by making us human.
> If we ever become human, we become images of God.[1]

NOTES

Introduction

1. *Gaudium et Spes, Vatican Council II Constitutions, Decrees, Declarations.* Austin Flannery, O.P., ed. (New York: Costello, 1996).
2. Gerald G. May, *Will and Spirit: A Contemplative Psychology* (San Francisco: Harper & Row, 1982).
3. Daniel J. Levinson, *Seasons of a Man's Life* (New York: Knopf, 1978); *Seasons of a Woman's Life* (New York: Knopf, 1996).
4. *Sacred Space: The Prayer Book* (Notre Dame, Ind.: Ave Maria, 2000), p. 135.
5. Prayer of Ignatius of Loyola, available at www.quotecatholic.com.

Chapter One

1. Meister Eckhart, quoted in *Passion for Creation: The Earth-Honoring Spirituality of Meister Eckhart,* Matthew Fox, ed. (Rochester, Vt.: Inner Traditions, 2002).
2. Levinson, *Seasons of a Man's Life,* pp. 90–97; *Seasons of a Woman's Life,* pp. 238–240.
3. Levinson, *Seasons of a Woman's Life,* p. xx.
4. Levinson, *Seasons of a Woman's Life,* p. 83.
5. Levinson, *Seasons of a Woman's Life,* pp. 46–56.
6. Levinson, *Seasons of a Woman's Life,* p. 56.
7. Levinson, *Seasons of a Woman's Life,* p. 93.
8. Quotes from the conference, "Seasons of Life, Seasons of Faith" will be hereinafter cited as "Conference Questionnaire."
9. Conference Questionnaire.
10. Conference Questionnaire.
11. Mike Hayes, *Googling God: The Religious Landscape of People in their 20s and 30s* (New York: Paulist, 2007).
12. Conference Questionnaire.
13. Conference Questionnaire.
14. Conference Questionnaire.
15. Levinson, *Seasons of a Woman's Life,* p. 365.
16. Conference Questionnaire.
17. Conference Questionnaire.
18. Conference Questionnaire.

19. Levinson, *Seasons of a Woman's Life*, pp. 121–122.

20. Claire A. Etaugh and Judith S. Bridges, *The Psychology of Women: A Lifespan Perspective* (Boston: Allyn and Bacon, 2000), p. 162.

21. Conference Questionnaire.

22. Levinson, *Seasons of a Woman's Life*, p. 402.

23. Conference Questionnaire.

24. Conference Questionnaire.

25. Conference Questionnaire.

26. Mother Teresa, *The Joy of Loving* (New York: Penguin, 2000), p. 65.

27. *Stewardship: A Disciple's Response.* A Summary of the U.S. Bishops' Pastoral Letter on Stewardship (Washington, D.C.: National Conference of Catholic Bishops, 1992).

28. Conference Questionnaire.

29. Etty Hillesum, *An Interrupted Life and Letters from Westerbork* (New York: Holt, 1996).

30. Robert Morneau, available at www.spiritualityandpractice.com/books/excerpts.php?id=19410.

31. Margaret Silf, *Inner Compass: An Invitation to Ignatian Spirituality* (Chicago: Loyola, 1999), p. 196.

Chapter Two

1. Dante Alighieri, *Inferno*, I,1–3.

2. Carl Jung, "Stages of Life," *The Portable Jung* (New York: Penguin, 1971), pp. 16–17. Other books that have influenced my presentation on Jung are Eugene C. Bianchi, *Aging as a Spiritual Journey* (New York: Crossroad, 1982); and John Welch, O.CARM., *Spiritual Pilgrims: Carl Jung and Teresa of Avila* (New York: Paulist, 1982).

3. Levinson, *Seasons of a Man's Life*, p. 23. Many of the ideas in this section find their origin in the two books by Levinson, *Seasons of a Man's Life* and *Seasons of a Woman's Life*. I will footnote only specific quotes from these two sources.

4. Levinson, *Seasons of a Woman's Life*, p. 354.

5. Unpublished manuscript.

6. Conference Questionnaire.

7. Conference Questionnaire.

8. Levinson, *Seasons of a Woman's Life*, pp. 380–381.
9. Conference Questionnaire.
10. Conference Questionnaire.
11. Conference Questionnaire.
12. Conference Questionnaire.
13. Levinson, *Seasons of a Woman's Life*, p. 372.
14. Levinson, *Seasons of a Woman's Life*, p. 381.
15. Conference Questionnaire.
16. Conference Questionnaire.
17. Conference Questionnaire.
18. See Elizabeth Johnson, *Truly Our Sister: A Theology of Mary in the Communion of Saints* (New York: Continuum, 2003); Catherine Mowry LaCugna, *God For Us: The Trinity and Christian Life* (San Francisco: HarperSanFrancisco, 1991). For a symposium of women presenting papers representing differing points of view, see *The Church Women Want: Catholic Women in Dialogue*, Elizabeth Johnson, ed. (New York: Crossroad, 2002).
19. Conference Questionnaire.
20. John Kirvan, *God Hunger: Discovering the Mystic in All of Us* (Notre Dame, Ind.: Sorin, 1999), p. 43.
21. Unpublished manuscript.
22. My presentation of John of the Cross has been influenced by the following resources: Iain Matthew, *The Impact of God: Soundings from St. John of the Cross* (London: Hodder & Stoughton, 1995); Gerald May, M.D. *The Dark Night of the Soul: A Psychiatrist Explores the Connection Between Darkness and Spiritual Growth* (San Francisco: HarperSanFrancisco, 2005); John Welch, O. CARM., *When Gods Die: An Introduction to John of the Cross* (New York: Paulist, 1990); Constance Fitzgerald, "Impasse and the Dark Night" in *Women's Spirituality*, 2nd edition, JoAnn Wolski Conn, ed. (New York: Paulist, 1996).
23. Conference Questionnaire.
24. Gerald May, *The Dark Night of the Soul*, p. 59.
25. Clare Wagner, *Awakening to Prayer: A Woman's Perspective* (Cincinnati: St. Anthony Messenger Press, 2009), p. 46.
26. Conference Questionnaire.
27. Conference Questionnaire.

28. Anne Morrow Lindbergh, *Gift from the Sea* (New York: Pantheon, 2003), pp. 78–79.

29. Margaret Silf, *Inner Compass*, p. 45.

30. John of the Cross, "The Ascent of Mount Carmel," in *Selected Writings* (New York: Paulist, 1987), pp. 55–56.

31. *Sacred Space*, p. 47.

Chapter Three

1. Lillian Hellman, quoted in Anita Spencer, *Seasons* (New York: Paulist, 1978), p. 45.

2. Kathleen Norris, *Acedia & Me. A Marriage, Monks and a Writer's Life* (New York: Penguin, 2008), pp. 113–114.

3. Levinson, *Seasons of a Woman's Life*, p. 33.

4. Conference Questionnaire.

5. Conference Questionnaire.

6. Quoted in Spencer, *Seasons*, p. 50.

7. Robert Ellsberg, *Blessed Among All Women: Women Saints, Prophets, and Witnesses for our Time* (New York: Crossroad, 2005), p. 2.

8. Conference Questionnaire.

9. As quoted in Welch, *Spiritual Pilgrims*, p. 120.

10. Jolande Jacobi, *Masks of the Soul* (Grand Rapids: Eerdmans, 1976), p. 54.

11. Levinson, *Seasons of a Woman's Life*, p. 167.

12. Conference Questionnaire.

13. Dr. Ronald Modras, *Ignatian Humanism: A Dynamic Spirituality for the 21st Century* (Chicago: Loyola, 2004), p. 238.

14. Karl Rahner, *The Practice of Faith: A Handbook of Contemporary Spirituality*. Karl Lehmann and Albert Raffelt, eds., John Griffiths, trans. (New York: Crossroad, 1986), pp. 80–81.

15. Hillesum, p. 231.

16. Levinson, *Seasons of a Man's Life*, pp. 239–243.

17. Robert Kegan, PH. D. *The Evolving Self. Problems and Process in Human Development* (Cambridge: Harvard University Press, 1982).

18. Gail Sheehy, "Hillaryland at War," *Vanity Fair* (August, 2008), pp. 1–7.

19. Sheehy, p. 7.

20. John Paul II, *The Genius of Women* (Washington, D.C.: USCCB, 1997), pp.

1–18. See also, Sara Butler, M.S.B.T. "Embodiment: Women and Men: Equal and Complementary," *The Church Women Want: Catholic Women in Dialogue.* Elizabeth A. Johnson, ed. (New York: Crossroad, 2002), pp. 33–35.

21. John Paul II, *The Genius of Women,* pp. 1–18.

22. Elizabeth Johnson, *Truly Our Sister: A Theology of Mary in the Communion of Saints* (New York: Continuum, 2003), pp. 52–53.

23. Johnson, p. 64.

24. Levinson, *Seasons of a Man's Life,* pp. 239–243.

25. Erik Erikson, *Identity, Youth and Crisis* (New York: Norton, 1968), pp. 96–106.

26. Erik Erikson, *The Life Cycle Completed: A Review* (New York: Norton, 1982), p. 103.

27. Conference Questionnaire.

28. Anne Morrow Lindberg, *Gift From the Sea,* p. 44.

29. Ron Modras, *Ignatian Humanism,* p. 296.

30. A prayer attributed to Teresa of Avila.

31. Martin Laird, *Into the Silent Land: A Guide to the Christian Practice of Contemplation* (New York: Oxford University Press, 2006).

32. Laird, p. 8.

33. Conference Questionnaire.

34. Norris, *Acedia and Me,* pp. 89–90.

35. John J. Kirvan, *Let Nothing Disturb You: A Journey to the Center of the Soul with Teresa of Avila* (Notre Dame, Ind.: Ave Maria, 2004), p. 7.

Chapter Four

1. May Sarton, *Collected Poems 1930–1973* (New York: Norton, 1974), pp. 409–410.

2. Conference Questionnaire.

3. Erikson, *The Life Cycle Completed,* pp. 62–63.

4. Erikson, *Vital Involvement in Old Age* (New York: Norton, 1986), p. 103.

5. Conference Questionnaire.

6. Pamela D. Blair, PH. D. *The Next Fifty Years: Guide for Women at Midlife and Beyond* (New York: Hampton, 2005), p. xiii.

7. Erik Erikson, *Vital Involvement in Old Age,* p. 58.

8. Conference Questionnaire.
9. Conference Questionnaire.
10. Conference Questionnaire.
11. Blair, *The Next Fifty Years*, p. 178.
12. Helen Hayes, *Helen Hayes* (New York: Doubleday, 1984).
13. Conference Questionnaire.
14. Blair, *The Next Fifty Years*, p. 227.
15. Blair, *The Next Fifty Years*, p. 224.
16. Charles J. Fahey, "Spiritual Well-Being of the Elderly in Relation to God," as quoted in Bianci, *Aging as a Spiritual Journey*, p. 167.
17. Conference Questionnaire.
18. James Martin, S.J., *My Life with the Saints* (Chicago: Loyola, 2006), p. 219.
19. Conference Questionnaire.
20. Conference Questionnaire.
21. Conference Questionnaire.
22. Conference Questionnaire.
23. Conference Questionnaire.
24. Quoted in Blair, *The Next Fifty Years*, p. 217.
25. Bianci, *Aging as a Spiritual Journey*, p. 251.
26. Erik Erikson, "Reflections on Dr. Borg's Life Cycle," *Adulthood.* (New York: Norton, 1978), p. 26.
27. Conference Questionnaire.
28. Daniel Goleman, "Erikson, In His Own Old Age, Expands His View of Life," available at http://www.nytimes.com/books/99/08/22/specials/erikson–old.html.
29. Goleman, p. 2.
30. Jon Meacham, "Pilgrim's Progress," *Newsweek* (August 14, 2006), pp. 37–44.
31. Conference Questionnaire.
32. Conference Questionnaire.
33. Sister Janet Ruffing, *Spiritual Direction*, pp. 108–109.
34. Teresa of Avila, *Life*, chapter five.
35. Teresa of Avila, *The Interior Castle* (New York: Paulist, 1979), I:8.
36. Conference Questionnaire.
37. Teresa of Avila, *The Way of Perfection*, pp. 83–84.

38. Teresa of Avila, *The Interior Castle* III, chap. 1, no. 5.

39. Conference Questionnaire.

40. Conference Questionnaire.

41. Teresa of Avila, *The Interior Castle*, III, chap. 1, no. 6.

42. Conference Questionnaire.

43. Conference Questionnaire.

44. Conference Questionnaire.

45. Gillian T.W. Ahlgren, *Entering Teresa of Avila's Interior Castle* (Mahwah, N.Y.: Paulist, 2005), p. 50.

46. Conference Questionnaire.

47. Teresa of Avila, *The Interior Castle*, IV, chap. 3.

48. Teresa of Avila, *The Interior Castle*, V, chap. 6.

49. Ahlgren, pp. 49–50.

50. Teresa of Avila, *The Interior Castle*, VI, chap. 2.

51. Teresa of Avila, *The Interior Castle*, VII, chap. 2, no. 3.

52. Teresa of Avila, *The Interior Castle*, VII, chap. 4, no. 7.

53. Constance Fitzgerald, "Transformation in Wisdom," in K. Culligan and R. Jordan, eds., *Carmelite Studies VIII: Carmel and Contemplation* (Washington, D.C.: ICS, 2000), pp. 309–330.

54. John of the Cross, *The Dark Night*, in *Collected Works of St. John of the Cross*. Kieran Kavanaugh, O.C.D., trans. (Washington, D.C.: ICS, 1979).

55. Thérèse of Lisieux, *Story of a Soul*, in *The Autobiography of St. Thérèse of Lisieux* (Washington, D.C.: ICS, 1996), pp. 212–213.

56. Thérèse of Lisieux, *Story of a Soul* p. 214.

57. Sister Margaret R. Brennan, I.H.M., *What Was There for Me Once: A Memoir* (Toronto: Novalis, 2009), pp. 164–165.

58. Brennan, pp. 164–165.

59. Brennan, p. 165.

60. John of the Cross, *Selected Writings* (New York: Paulist, 1987), p. 294.

61. Conference Questionnaire.

62. A reflection attributed to Pedro Arrupe, S.J., from an unpublished lecture.

63. John Kirvan, *God Hunger*, p. 161.

Conclusion

1. Unpublished class notes from Father Michael Scanlon, professor of Christian anthropology, Washington Theological Union.

Hillesum, Etty, 61–62
holiness, and wholeness, growth in, xv
Holy Spirit
    and grace, 60
    as transformation of desire, 42
hope, in healing process of dark
    night, 110
human development
    Kegan's model of, 64–65, 67, 68
    and spiritual growth, xx
    See also adult development, life
    cycle
humanism, Ignatian, 74

individuation, 26, 50
inner selves
    relationship with, 26
    turning inward, 27–28
institutions, reappraising role of,
    35–38
integrity, vs. despair, 90–92
intentional faith, 100–101
The Interior Castle, 94, 95–97, 111
interpersonal faith, during spring,
    5–10
Into the Silent Land, 75

Jacobi, Jolande, 57
Jesus
    doing "in memory of," 73–74
    God revealed in, 60
    as model for integrating prayer and
    action, 17–18
John of the Cross, 10 16, 104 111
John Paul II, and complementary
    approach to Christian personhood,
    66–67, 68–69, 78
Johnson, Sister Elizabeth, 67–68
Jung, Carl, 25–37, 50, 56–58

Kegan, Robert, 63–64, 67, 68

Laird, Martin, 75
legacy, 53, 55

Levinson, Daniel, xiv, xvi–xix, 1–4,
    10–11, 27, 28, 33, 34–35, 50, 51,
    53, 62–63, 82
life cycle
    chart, xviii, xxiii
    seasonal nature of, xix
life structures
    building around dream, 2–5
    crisis during midlife, 32–35
    modifying during midlife, 29–32
    stable and transitional periods
    within, xvii, 10–11
Lindbergh, Anne Morrow, 46, 72
losses, 88–90
love
    four stages of, 109
    of God and neighbor, unity of, 113
    God's, 94–95
    in healing process of dark night, 10
    passionate, and love of Jesus, 6

mansions, Teresa of Avila's concept of,
    95–104
marriage
    for career women, 11–12
    disappointment with, 34
    as early adulthood dream, 2–3, 11
    in final phase of life, 84–85
    reappraising, 30
    spiritual, 103
    See also family
masculine/feminine polarity, 50,
    62–69, 77
"masculine" qualities, 29
materialism, 15 16
May, Gerald, xv, 104
meaning, concern with, 27–28
memories
    making, 83–88
    purification of, 106–107
menopause, as example of destruc-
    tion/creation polarity, 58–59
Merton, Thomas, 39
middle-aged women, stereotypes,
    52–53

Called to Holiness Series

A groundbreaking eight-volume series on women's spirituality, *Called to Holiness: Spirituality for Catholic Women* will cover the many diverse facets of a woman's interior life and help her discover how God works with her and through her. An ideal resource for a woman seeking to find how God charges the moments of her life—from spirituality itself, to the spirituality of social justice, the spirituality of grieving the loss of a loved one, the creation and nurturing of families, the mentoring of young adult Catholic women, to recognition of the shared wisdom of women in the middle years—this series can be used by individuals or in groups. Far from the cloister or monastery, these books find God in the midst of a woman's everyday life and help her to find and celebrate God's presence day to day and acknowledge her own gifts as an ordinary "theologian." The books can be used independently or together for individual discussion or group faith sharing. Each book will include gathering rituals, reflection questions, and annotated bibliographies.

Making Sense of God
A Woman's Perspective
Elizabeth A. Dreyer

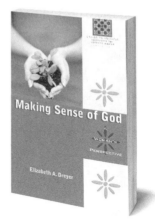

The moment is ripe for ordinary Catholic women to "do Christian theology." Times such as these challenge us to be holy, to be alive in the Spirit, to summon the energy, and make the commitment to help one another grow spiritually. Now is the time for Catholic women to make sense of God.

In this introductory volume to the *Called to Holiness* series, Catholic theologian Elizabeth Dreyer encourages us to acknowledge our dignity, harvest our gifts and empower all women in church and society. Dreyer helps us to shape what we think about God, justice, love, prayer, family life, the destiny of humanity and the entire universe.

Paper, 128 pp.
Order #B16884
ISBN 978-0-86716-884-6
$11.95

Living a Spirituality of Action
A Woman's Perspective
Joan Mueller

"Own your gifts and use them to make the world a better place," Catholic theologian Joan Mueller writes. In this practical book she provides us with ideas and encouragement to live and act with courage to change the world, even if our actions are sometimes small.

This is a book for all who hear about hungry people living in the park and decide to make sandwiches, who volunteer to teach children to read, who raise money to change systems that provide substandard care to the vulnerable, who can imagine a mothered world. Mueller invites us to discuss and embrace our shared wisdom.

Paper, 112 pp.
Order #B16885
ISBN 978-0-86716-885-3
$11.95

Grieving With Grace
A Woman's Perspective
Dolores R. Leckey

There are many ways in which the course of our daily lives can be altered—illness, change in residence, loss of employment, and death of loved one: These alterations can require dramatic and even subtle changes in our everyday living, limit our options and force us to choose different priorities.

Dolores Leckey knows firsthand that the death of a spouse changes forever the rhythms of life at all levels—body, mind, and soul. In this moving and personal narrative that includes entries from her journal, she shares with us her own shift in consciousness, in the way she sees God, herself and the world after her husband's death. She offers us consolation and hope.

Paper, 112 pp.
Order #B16888
ISBN 978-0-86716-888-4
$11.95

Awakening to Prayer
A Woman's Perspective
Clare Wagner

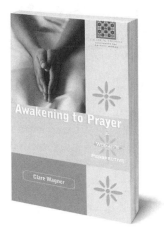

The word "prayer" is almost as generic as *food* or *book*, says Clare Wagner in *Awakening to Prayer: A Woman's Perspective,* and the varieties of prayer forms are countless. In this best and worst of times, Wagner writes, it is intriguing to ponder how women of the twenty-first century pray and enter into a relationship with Holy Presence.

To help us see anew, she draws on the wisdom of the Scriptures, the insights of the mystics, and the experience of ordinary, vibrant women and men living in our midst. She offers suggestions of words to use and rituals to experience to help us awaken to prayer.

Paper, 112 pp.
Order #B16892
ISBN 978-0-86716-892-1
$11.95

Embracing Latina Spirituality
A Woman's Perspective
Michelle A. Gonzalez

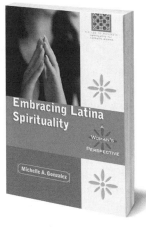

Latinas treat the sacred in ways that are similar to the ways we treat those we encounter every day: They converse with statues of saints and Mary, leave them flowers and light candles to persuade them to gain favor for us, and become angry when prayers are not answered. These everyday aspects of Latina spirituality reflect a strong sense of family and community that we can embrace as a refreshing spiritual alternative to the individualism that permeates our society.

Entering into the world of Latina spirituality offers new ways to understand self and community and to approach prayer, diversity, and the struggle against oppression. Latina spirituality provides us an entry point into true unity.

Paper, 112 pp.
Order #B16886
ISBN 978-0-86716-886-0
$11.95

Creating New Life, Nurturing Families
A Woman's Perspective
Sidney Callahan

Digging deeply into the various dimensions of women's journeys and discussing love and marriage, sex, mothering, work, and transforming joy amidst suffering, Callahan shows how a woman's commitment to the well-being of her husband and children is a participation in the very life of the Trinity. She explores the many ways that a wife and mother pours out her love for her family, as Christ poured out his love for us, and shows how that humbling of yourself, day after day, ensures that God's message of hope and salvation will be passed on to generations to come.

Paper, 144 pp.
Order #B16893
ISBN 978-0-86716-893-8
$11.95

Finding My Voice
A Young Woman's Perspective
Beth M. Knobbe

Finding My Voice: A Young Woman's Perspective will help you find answers to life's persistent questions: Who am I? Where am I going? Who is going with me?

Beth M. Knobbe understands firsthand the ups and downs of being 20-something, the desire to belong, the longing to love and be loved. She knows the mysteries and realities of getting a career off the ground, the subtle temptations to conform to what the world wants and the ads say you must be, and the challenges you face to make people understand that you have a voice and you have something meaningful to say.

Paper, 160 pp.
Order #B16894
ISBN 978-0-86716-894-5
$11.95

ABOUT THE AUTHOR

Patricia Cooney Hathaway is associate professor of spirituality and systematic theology at Sacred Heart Major Seminary in Detroit. She earned a doctorate in systematic theology from the Catholic University of America. She speaks nationally on the topics of theology, spirituality, and human and spiritual adult development, and is a regular contributor to *Mosaic* magazine and other publications. She is married to Thomas Hathaway, and they are the parents of Thomas and Victoria.